The Limits of DeFi for Financial Inclusion

LESSONS FROM ASEAN

OECD

BETTER POLICIES FOR BETTER LIVES

This document, as well as any data and map included herein, are without prejudice to the status of or sovereignty over any territory, to the delimitation of international frontiers and boundaries and to the name of any territory, city or area.

The statistical data for Israel are supplied by and under the responsibility of the relevant Israeli authorities. The use of such data by the OECD is without prejudice to the status of the Golan Heights, East Jerusalem and Israeli settlements in the West Bank under the terms of international law.

Please cite this publication as:
OECD (2024), *The Limits of DeFi for Financial Inclusion: Lessons from ASEAN*, OECD Publishing, Paris, https://doi.org/10.1787/f00a0c7f-en.

ISBN 978-92-64-52689-1 (print)
ISBN 978-92-64-65199-9 (pdf)
ISBN 978-92-64-57179-2 (HTML)
ISBN 978-92-64-80851-5 (epub)

Photo credits: Cover © anyaberkut/Getty Images.

Corrigenda to OECD publications may be found on line at: www.oecd.org/about/publishing/corrigenda.htm.

Foreword

This report examines the limitations of DeFi and crypto-asset activity at the current stage of market development for the promotion of financial inclusion. It provides examples from ASEAN economies and beyond and provides policy recommendations.

The report has been drafted by Iota Kaousar Nassr and Seohyun Kim under the supervision of Fatos Koc and with oversight from Serdar Çelik from the Division of Capital Markets and Financial Institutions Division of the OECD Directorate for Financial and Enterprise Affairs. Eva Abbott and Meral Gedik provided editorial and communication support.

The report supports the work of the OECD Committee on Financial Markets, chaired by Aerdt Houben and was discussed by the Committee in October 2023. The report was approved and declassified by the OECD Committee on Financial Markets on 2 February 2023.

The authors gratefully acknowledge valuable input and feedback provided by the following individuals and organisations: Béranger Butruille, Banque de France; Adam Głogowski and Paweł Gąsiorowski , National Bank of Poland; Sooa Kim, Korean Financial Services Commission; Hyunyeol Kim, Korea Institute of Finance; Eleftheria Kostika, Bank of Greece; Borut Poljšak, Bank of Slovenia; Paull Randt, US Treasury; Tatu Rasanen, Bank of Finland; Mai Santamaria, Jefferson Vieira and Mark Curran, Department of Finance, Ireland; Andreas Schrimpf, Bank for International Settlements; as well as Philip Gant, Harvard Asia Center and Flore-Anne Messy and Max Bulakovskiy from the OECD.

The report was supported through funding by the Government of Korea.

Table of contents

Foreword 3

Executive summary 7

1 DeFi and crypto-asset market trends in ASEAN 9
1.1. Decentralised finance market trends in ASEAN 9
1.2. Breakdown of decentralised finance activity by ASEAN Member State 11
1.3. Types of crypto-assets in ASEAN 15
1.4. The importance of stablecoins in the ASEAN ecosystem 16
1.5. DeFi protocol activity in Asia 18
Notes 22

2 The limits of DeFi for the democratisation of finance 23
2.1. Decentralised finance and the false promise of democratisation of finance 23

3 FinTech applications with potential benefits for financial inclusion 33
3.1. Regulated DLT-based finance: tokenisation and regulated digital assets 34
Notes 38

4 Policy considerations 39
4.1. A rapidly evolving regulatory framework for DeFi and crypto-asset activity to mitigate risks and protect investors and markets 39
4.2. Policies to support a safe digital transformation and the development of FinTech that can contribute to financial inclusion 41
Note 43

Annex A. Aggregate net flows across geographies 44

Annex B. Aggregate AMS Country data 45

References 55

FIGURES

Figure 1.1. Diverse level of decentralised finance activity in ASEAN 9
Figure 1.2. Crypto-asset activity in ASEAN 10
Figure 1.3. Significant levels of crypto-asset activity in many ASEAN Member States 12
Figure 1.4. Share of respondents in AMS who have used or owned crypto-assets from 2019 to 2023 12
Figure 1.5. Share of respondents of Play-to-earn gaming adoption in ASEAN as of 2022 13
Figure 1.6. Bitcoin mining activity 14
Figure 1.7. Breakdown of crypto-asset activity in ASEAN by type of asset 16
Figure 1.8. Claimed use cases of so-called stablecoin arrangements 17
Figure 1.9. Cumulative stablecoin flows in ASEAN from 2020 to 2022 17
Figure 1.10. DeFi and crypto-asset market evolution 18
Figure 1.11. DeFi ASEAN flows 18
Figure 1.12. Inflows of Ether to DeFi by country in 2022 19
Figure 1.13. Increasing part of crypto-asset trading occurring in DEXs 20
Figure 1.14. Aggregate net flows across geographies from 2020 to 2023 20
Figure 1.15. Yearly Crypto-asset flows to ASEAN from 2022 to 2022 21
Figure 2.1. Professional investors dominate decentralised finance activity in East Asia from July 2019 to June 2020 24
Figure 2.2. Negligible minority of DeFi transactions come from retail investors from June 2020 to 31 January 2023 25
Figure 2.3. Inflow of funds to DeFi by type of investor from June 1, 2020 to January 31, 2023 25
Figure 2.4. Average trade size in DEXs vs. CEXsof March 1, 2023 – July 22, 2023 26
Figure 2.5. Number of retail holders of mainstream crypto-assets and stablecoins from 2020 to H1 2023 27
Figure 2.6. Small Bitcoin holders net buyers during the crypto winter, large holders sellers as of end September 2022 28
Figure 2.7. Total crypto-asset flows by time horizon profile 29
Figure 2.8. Stablecoin usage in DeFi activity one of the major current use cases globally 30
Figure 2.9. USDC trading volume on DEXs vs. CEXs 30
Figure 2.10. USDC liquidity deposited on ETH-based DeFi lending protocols 31
Figure 2.11. Correlation between Stablecoin and Altcoin in ASEAN from 2020 to 2022 31
Figure 2.12. Stablecoin market breakdown from July 2020 to July 2023 32
Figure 2.13. Stablecoins holding distribution by type of holder 32
Figure 3.1. Underserved part of ASEAN population and banked status of FinTech customers 33
Figure 3.2. SiriHub real estate tokenisation transaction structure 35
Figure 4.1. FSB High-level Recommendations for the Regulation, Supervision and Oversight of Crypto-asset Activities and Markets and "Global Stablecoin" Arrangements 41

Figure A A.1. Cumulative aggregate net flows across geographies from each year 44
Figure A B.1. Breakdown of crypto-asset activity by type of asset and Crypto-asset flows to Brunei Darussalam 45
Figure A B.2. Breakdown of crypto-asset activity by type of asset and Crypto-asset flows to Cambodia 46
Figure A B.3. Breakdown of crypto-asset activity by type of asset and Crypto-asset flows to Indonesia 47
Figure A B.4. Breakdown of crypto-asset activity by type of asset and Crypto-asset flows to Lao People's Democratic Republic 48
Figure A B.5. Breakdown of crypto-asset activity by type of asset and Crypto-asset flows to Malaysia 49
Figure A B.6. Breakdown of crypto-asset activity by type of asset and Crypto-asset flows to Myanmar 50
Figure A B.7. Breakdown of crypto-asset activity by type of asset and Crypto-asset flows to Philippines 51
Figure A B.8. Breakdown of crypto-asset activity by type of asset and Crypto-asset flows to Singapore 52
Figure A B.9. Breakdown of crypto-asset activity by type of asset and Crypto-asset flows to Thailand 53
Figure A B.10. Breakdown of crypto-asset activity by type of asset and Crypto-asset flows to Viet Nam 54

TABLES

Table 4.1. Existing regulation of crypto-assets in ASEAN 40

BOXES

Box 1.1. The Terra-LUNA implosion and its impact on retail investors 11
Box 1.2. Crypto-asset mining and the negative environmental footprint of crypto-asset activity 15
Box 3.1. Real estate tokenisation: The example of Thailand 35
Box 3.2. Singapore framework for digital token offerings 36
Box 3.3. Use of artificial intelligence-based models for credit scoring: the case of Viet Nam 37
Box 3.4. Strengthening transaction safety through AI tools promotes consumer trust: the case of AI-assisted mule account detection 38

Executive summary

The ASEAN region is grappling with two seemingly contradictory forces: on one hand, a large part of the population (more than half) being underbanked or unbanked, and on the other hand, a young and digitally savvy population with high mobile internet connectivity. The digitally savvy part of the population is also the most comfortable with using crypto-assets, including stablecoins, and Decentralised Finance protocols (DeFi) (together referred to as decentralised finance).

These characteristics are consistent with the sizeable activity of ASEAN member states (AMS) in decentralised finance markets. Thailand, the Philippines and Viet Nam were among the top 10 crypto-asset adopters globally in 2022, while Malaysia is one of the nine countries with the largest Bitcoin mining activity on its territory. "Play-to-earn" blockchain-based gaming applications involving crypto-assets lured in many young individuals in the Philippines and other AMS, although these activities proved short-lived.

Important crypto-asset flows per capita have been recorded in almost all AMS, with peaks in activity coinciding with high crypto-asset valuations, indicating speculative forces driving these markets to a large extent. The Bitcoin and stablecoins dominate decentralised finance activity in the region, following global trends in the preference for such 'mainstream' crypto-assets. Although it is difficult to obtain accurate statistics on the geographic breakdown of DeFi activity, industry estimates of aggregate flows indicate important DeFi protocol activity in Asia for the period 2022 - H1 2023.

Part of this activity could be attributed to ASEAN users seeking to participate in these markets for their purported benefits regarding financial inclusion. Indeed, crypto-asset and DeFi protocols have been marketed as a tool to promote the democratisation of finance by replacing legacy centralised and intermediated finance with peer-to-peer disintermediated markets. These markets, however, involve the unregulated or non-compliant provision of financial services, depending on the jurisdiction, and thus expose investors to important risks in the absence of traditional safeguards for investor protection, market integrity and financial stability.

In practice, at the current stage of development of these markets, decentralised finance has failed to deliver on the promise of democratisation of finance, instead exposing retail participants to disproportionately high risks and loss of investment without recourse. The Asian region was at the epicenter of the 2022-23 crypto-asset market downturn (the 'crypto winter'), as the first major collapse of the domino failures was the Terra Luna implosion. The impact of crypto-asset firm failures on many retail holders was disproportionally high compared to large investors who have managed to cover some of their losses. In fact, small wallet-holders appear to be net buyers in the aftermath of the failures, against larger wallet-holders that offloaded their holdings early on.

Quantitative evidence from ASEAN suggests that professional and institutional investors (including centralised crypto-asset service providers) have been the most active participants of DeFi, and the share of professional activity as part of total volume is the highest in East Asia. Despite the prominence of professional investors, there are still sizeable amounts of retail users participating in these markets, and the number of small crypto-asset wallet holders has been increasing over the period 2020-H1 2023.

Speculative forces and a fear of missing out, rather than practical use-cases – such as to facilitate payments – have driven participation in these markets. The huge volatility of crypto-assets and the difficulty in valuing them make them unsuitable for payments purposes. When it comes to currently unregulated stablecoins, it is difficult to assess whether these have been used for real use cases, such as remittances, however, there are indications that these are heavily used either as a way to hedge against weak/volatile currencies or as a means of exchange within decentralised finance. Given that crypto-asset exchanges do not offer trading across all crypto-asset pairs, trading of small "altcoins" need to go through stablecoins, and this is also showcased by the high correlation between stablecoin and altcoin trading in ASEAN. The important risks associated with unregulated stablecoins (including unreliable reserves, unclear redemption rights and a lack of stability) make them outright unsuited for remittance use cases.

Retail participation in decentralised finance (particularly DeFi protocol activity) may also be more difficult due to its complexity, unregulated nature or the provision of uncompliant financial service provision and non-custodial nature. Despite the emergence of more user-friendly interfaces for access to these markets, they remain opaque and complex for the average retail user and involve complex leveraged trading strategies that are unfit for the uninitiated and non-tech-savvy retail user.

Despite its limitations in regard to the democratisation of finance, innovation associated with decentralised finance provided in a regulated and compliant form could offer possible benefits that may merit further exploration. Traditional financial market participants may adopt decentralised finance technologies and practices (e.g. atomic settlement of securities or post-trade/clearing disintermediation) to capture potential efficiencies and productivity gains in financial market infrastructure, and several experiments and pilots are underway globally – including in ASEAN – to explore such benefits. In the future, regulated or compliant crypto-assets and stablecoins may coexist with tokenised assets and tokenised forms of money (tokenised deposits and possibly central bank digital currencies (CBDCs)).

Other digital finance tools can act as important catalysts for financial inclusion in ASEAN, particularly when it comes to MSME financing. Thin file clients can be serviced through better calibration of lending risks, including through the deployment of AI-based models and big data for creditworthiness assessment. DLT-based finance and tokenisation can offer efficiencies by lowering the cost of servicing small size transactions. It can also allow for fractionalisation and offer new pathways for capital formation. Nevertheless, such innovative applications come with challenges and risks that need to be accounted for and mitigated.

ASEAN policymakers will need to consider ways to balance the opportunities of digital innovation in finance with the risks that these entails. ASEAN policymakers have been embracing the digital transformation of finance as an enabler for more efficient, inclusive and competitive markets. By fostering responsible and safe digital innovation in finance, policymakers can help unlock the potential for financial inclusion and productivity gains, while anticipating and addressing emerging risks for participants and the markets.

Digital finance-related policy frameworks need to be carefully calibrated and there is merit in harmonising policy approaches at the regional level, while ensuring consistency of domestic rules with global frameworks, such as the recent FSB framework for crypto-assets and stablecoin arrangements. Upskilling and capacity building among policymakers will be a prerequisite for the effective monitoring and oversight of these markets, while digital financial education could also be considered to strengthen user understanding and capacity. Nevertheless, FinTech on its own is no panacea, and the promotion of efforts and policies in traditional finance (e.g. digital IDs for banking KYC, credit bureaus) will need to continue to be pursued.

1 DeFi and crypto-asset market trends in ASEAN

The ASEAN region is home to the fastest growing internet user base, with a large proportion of the population being young urban citizens keen to adopt new technologies. This demographic group is most comfortable with using crypto-assets and participating in decentralised finance markets. This could partly explain the elevated levels of activity in markets for decentralised finance, comprising crypto-assets, including stablecoins, and DeFi protocol activity.

This chapter analyses DeFi and crypto-asset market activity in AMS in the period 2020-22 and examines trends, patterns and possible underlying drivers of peaks and troughs in activity in ASEAN.

1.1. Decentralised finance market trends in ASEAN

Activity in decentralised finance markets has been recorded in all ASEAN Member States, although the level of activity differs significantly across the countries, in line with the varying economic activity and diverse technological developments in the region (Figure 1.1). ASEAN economies are embracing digital technologies to varying degrees especially when it comes to institutional and infrastructural readiness, digital skills, and digital payments activities as evidenced by the ASEAN Digital Integration Index (ASEAN, 2021[1]).

Figure 1.1. Diverse level of decentralised finance activity in ASEAN

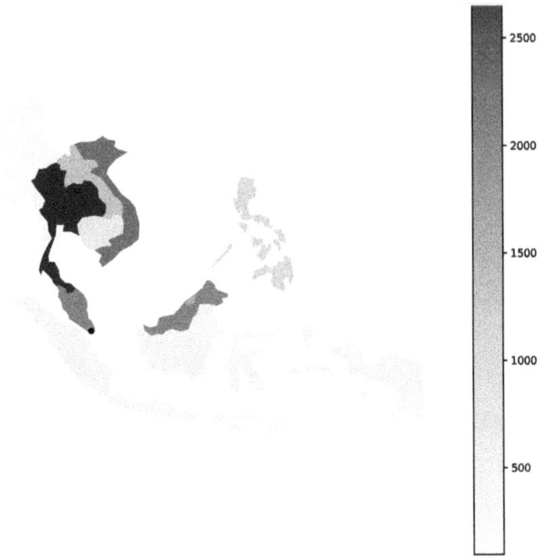

Note: Measured by crypto-asset flows per capita. Aggregate flows for the period 01/2020 to 05/2023, Average Population for 2020 and 2021.
Source: OECD based on Chainalysis flows and World Bank population data.

Crypto-asset flows towards ASEAN over the period 2020-22 follow a pattern that tracks to some extent the price evolution of Bitcoin (Figure 1.2). Indicatively, increased activity is recorded around October 2021, when Bitcoin reached a historical high of USD 61 525 (18 October, based on data from Chainalysis). This is not surprising as Bitcoin's price has been a major driver of overall decentralised finance activity globally. Feedback loops exist between Bitcoin, the price of which has driven much of the activity in the entire crypto-asset market, and the evolution of DeFi measured by the total value of such crypto-assets that is locked into smart contracts of DeFi protocols (OECD, 2022[2]).

Activity in ASEAN peaked in H2 2021, in line with global trends, and started subsiding in early 2022 at the onset of the crypto-asset market downturn (known as 'crypto winter') and in line with overall global trends in these markets (OECD, 2022[3]). Interestingly, crypto-asset flows towards ASEAN almost tripled in the aftermath of the Terra UST de-peg on 7 May 2023 (see Box 1.1). A total of USD 17bn of flows to ASEAN were recorded on 8 May 2022, compared to USD 6bn a week before. This could possibly be attributed to withdrawals from Terra-connected Anchor protocol in the wake of the UST de-peg, and to massive withdrawals from among similar DeFi protocols, among other things, by ASEAN-based investors.

Increased activity of decentralised finance markets in times when crypto-asset valuations are high is an indication of speculative forces driving these markets. Indeed, speculation and the potential for high returns are considered as the main drivers of investor interest and participation in this space (OECD, 2022[4]). There are no fundamental drivers of the surge in crypto-asset prices in what seems to be a market largely driven by speculation, given the very high returns that can be achieved due to the massive volatility of crypto-assets (excluding stablecoins), and the fear of missed returns (so-called fear of missing out or 'FOMO'). These forces are intensified given the extensive recycling of profits from some crypto-asset activities to others for example from mainstream crypto, such as Bitcoin, to DeFi protocols. The reflexive character of crypto-assets further intensifies these trends of common pattern in levels of activity asset types and regions.

Figure 1.2. Crypto-asset activity in ASEAN

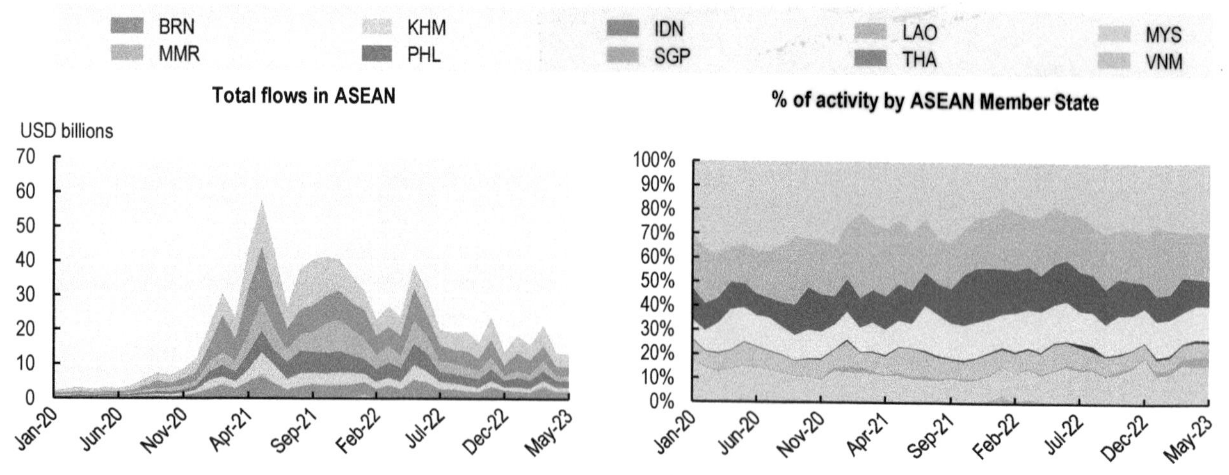

Note: Measured by total flows of crypto-assets in ASEAN. On a monthly basis, includes Bitcoin, Ether and Altcoin crypto-assets, and stablecoins.
Source: OECD based on Chainalysis data.

Box 1.1. The Terra-LUNA implosion and its impact on retail investors

The rise and fall of Terra's so-called stablecoin (UST) in a short time span is a useful case study exposing the risks involved in decentralised finance markets. UST issuance grew exponentially from 2% to 10% market share in one year with a USD 18 bn issuance volume as of April 2022.

On 7 May 2022, UST broke its peg with the US Dollar and suffered a run that resulted in significant losses for UST holders (UST declined from USD 0.99 to less than USD 0.13 in the course of five days). Some UST retail investors lost a significant part of their investment without any recourse for compensation. For example, in the case of Terra UST's implosion, 280 000 investors reportedly lost their investments (news1.kr, 2022[5]), as a result of whichnearly 4 400 retail investors have formed an association called 'the UST Restitution Group in pursuit of compensation from the Terra founder (FT, 2022[6]). Such investors appear to have been drawn into UST by the unsustainably high yields offered by protocols connected to UST (e.g. through the Anchor protocol) and with little understanding of the circular and reflexive character of these crypto-assets, which had no fundamental value.

The subsequent de-pegging of the largest so-called stablecoin at the time, Tether's USDT, which was reportedly backed by holdings of commercial paper, did not have an immediate observable contagion effect on short-term debt markets. However, it clearly highlighted the high interconnectedness within crypto-asset markets and gave rise to consideration of potential risks stemming from transmission channels to traditional markets, that did not materialise in the end. The UST implosion also highlighted the limits to creating unbacked private money, as well as the central role of trust and confidence in the market for crypto-assets. This is analogical to the importance that trust plays in traditional financial markets, where a sharp loss of confidence can affect the crypto-assets ecosystem. The failure of Terra's dominant stablecoin UST created contagion and had a domino effect in the broader crypto-asset market leading to the failure and bankruptcy of other crypto-asset firms such as Celsius and Three Arrows, ultimately culminating in the FTX collapse in November 2022.

Source: (OECD, 2022[3]; Nassr, 2022[7]).

1.2. Breakdown of decentralised finance activity by ASEAN Member State

Thailand recorded the highest crypto-asset flows per capita in the period 2020-22, followed by Malaysia and Viet Nam. Important crypto-asset flows per capita were also recorded in Brunei Darussalam, the Philippines and Lao PDR, and to a smaller extent in Indonesia, Cambodia and Singapore (Figure 1.1).

In absolute terms, Viet Nam has received the largest amount of cumulative crypto-asset inflows for the 2020-22 period examined, with a total of USD 0.19tn of crypto-inflows recorded in that period, followed by Thailand with USD 0.18tn (Figure 1.3). Singapore, the Philippines and Indonesia also recorded significant amounts of crypto inflows (USD 0.12tn, 0.11tn, and 0.09tn respectively). On the contrary, there has been little activity in Brunei Darussalam and Myanmar. Cambodia and Lao PDR recorded small absolute activity that, however, has been non-negligible on a per capital level (Figure 1.3).

Viet Nam, Thailand and the Philippines were among the top 10 crypto-asset adopters in 2022 according to some industry analysis (Chainalysis, 2022[8]). More than a third of the population in Malaysia, Viet Nam and Thailand have reported having used or owned crypto-assets based on an industry survey (Statista, 2023[9]).

Figure 1.3. Significant levels of crypto-asset activity in many ASEAN Member States

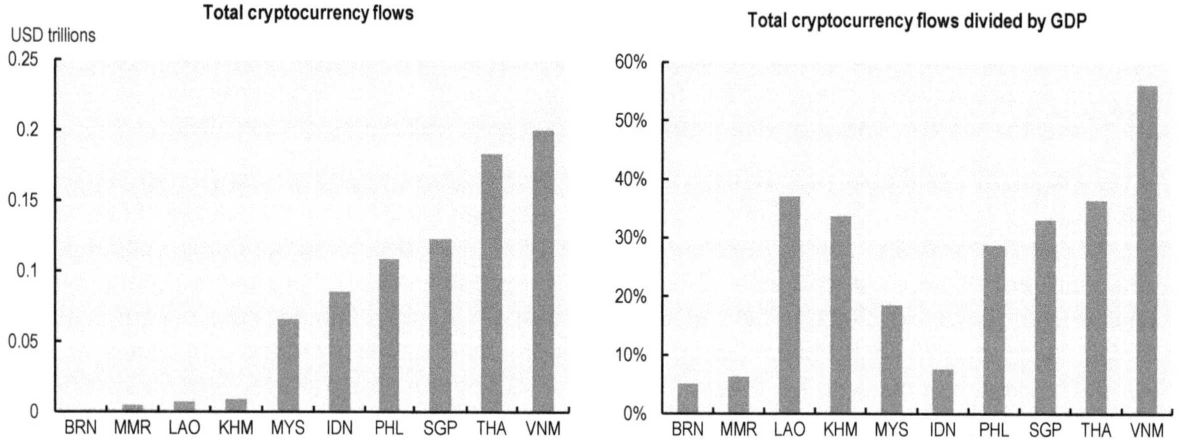

Note: Period from January 2020 to May 2023, average GDP 2020-21.
Source: OECD based on Chainalysis flows and World Bank population data.

Figure 1.4. Share of respondents in AMS who have used or owned crypto-assets from 2019 to 2023

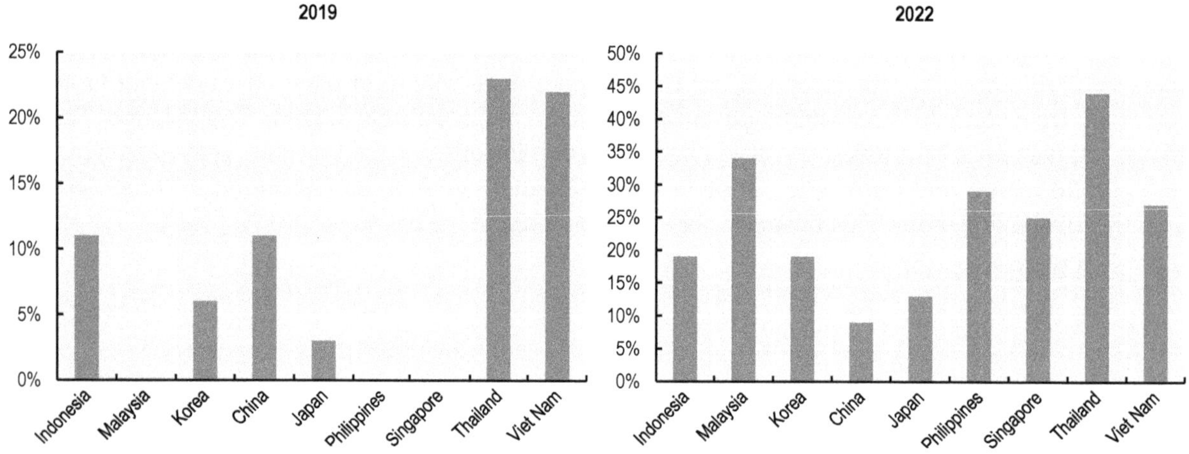

Note: Based on a sample of 2 000–12 000 respondents per country.
Source: Statista Global Consumer Survey.

1.2.1. The role of 'play-to-earn' blockchain-based gaming

Blockchain-based 'play-to-earn' gaming applications that involve crypto-assets may have fuelled the surge in new adopters in these three AMS. "Play-to-earn" gaming involves non-fungible tokens (NFTs) and relies on the use of Ethereum-based crypto-assets for the gaming economy. Viet Nam is the headquarter of ex-unicorn company Axie Infinity, a leading online gaming company, and its developing team Sky Mavis.[1] Thailand and the Philippines are also known as countries with increased blockchain-based gaming activity.

In-game rewards in crypto-assets have indeed lured in many young individuals who aimed at supplementing their income in some AMS. According to one estimate, out of 2.8m daily active users, 65% are estimated to come from South-east Asia with the majority being Filipinos (as of February 2022) (Knowledge Partners, 2022[10]). Rewards in crypto-assets within such systems depended on the value of such unbacked crypto-assets[2] and could therefore not be considered as a viable supplement to participants' income or conducive to financial inclusion in these countries. Anecdotal evidence suggests that participants from the region were left indebted as they could not earn enough to cover the borrowed funds for their initial participation in the platform (Time, 2022[11]).

Crypto-assets involved in blockchain-based gaming are exchanged in crypto-asset exchanges and carry the same risks as any crypto-asset, and as such, risks taken by participants involved are likely to outweigh any benefit of additional income for users. This includes risk of total loss of holdings through exploits or hacks, as was the case with the USD 540m hack that Axie Infinity suffered in March 2022 by hackers linked to North Korea (Elliptic, 2022[12]). Depending on the jurisdiction, they may also involve non-compliant provision of financial services or activity outside the regulatory perimeter, exposing participants to material risks (OECD, 2022[3]).

Increased crypto-asset activity in Malaysia and (to a lesser extent) Thailand can also be attributed to crypto-asset mining activity. Malaysia is one of the top 9 countries with crypto-mining activity and Thailand ranks 2nd of 10 ASEAN countries (see Figure 1.6). Crypto-mining provides a flow of newly-created Bitcoin in particular, and incentivises trading activity and the creation of an ecosystem around the mining activity.

Figure 1.5. Share of respondents of Play-to-earn gaming adoption in ASEAN as of 2022

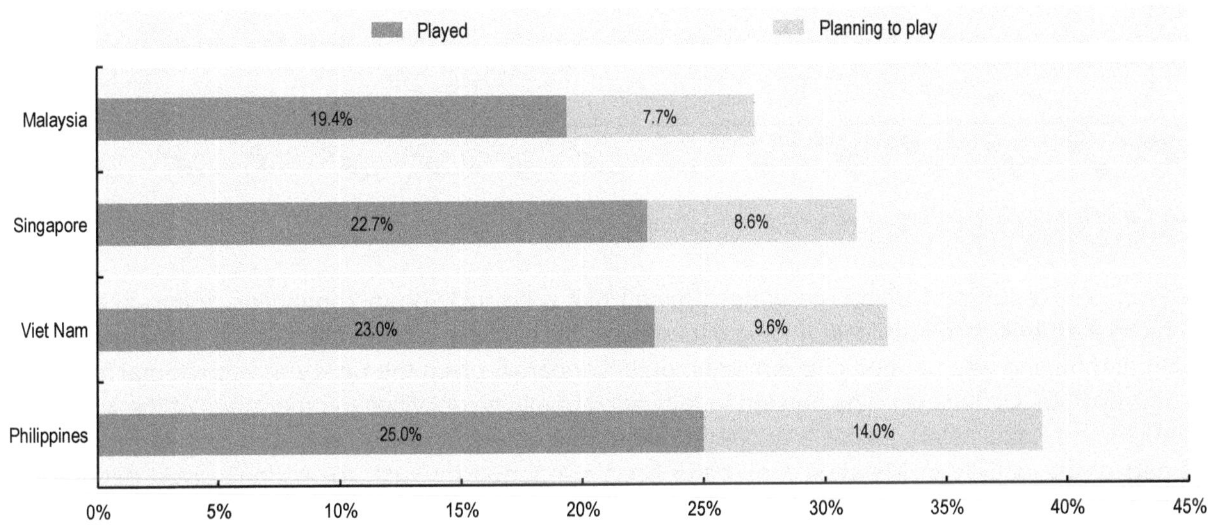

Source: (Finder, 2022[13]).

1.2.2. Crypto-mining activity in ASEAN

Evidence of crypto-asset mining activity has been recorded in 7 AMS, with the largest part of such activity happening in Malaysia and some non-negligible activity also taking place in Thailand. In fact, Malaysia is listed as one of the 9 countries with the largest Bitcoin mining activity as estimated by the Cambridge Bitcoin Electricity Consumption Index, accounting for 4.2% of global Bitcoin mining (Figure 1.6). Thailand accounts for 0.6% of global Bitcoin mining activity, and there is minor mining activity estimated to take place in Indonesia, Viet Nam, Philippines and Cambodia.

The main motive for crypto-asset mining is the associated financial rewards: mining revenues consist of the sum of transaction fees paid to miners, plus the market value of newly minted coins awarded to miners who successfully compete to record transactions to the blockchain. Holding all else equal, Bitcoin mining firms' profit margins increase when the price of the underlying crypto-asset increases, and therefore mining activity – and the corresponding energy consumption – is greater when the price of the underlying crypto-asset increases (OECD, 2022[14]). That explains the increase in activity in periods of crypto-asset market exuberance.

Figure 1.6. Bitcoin mining activity

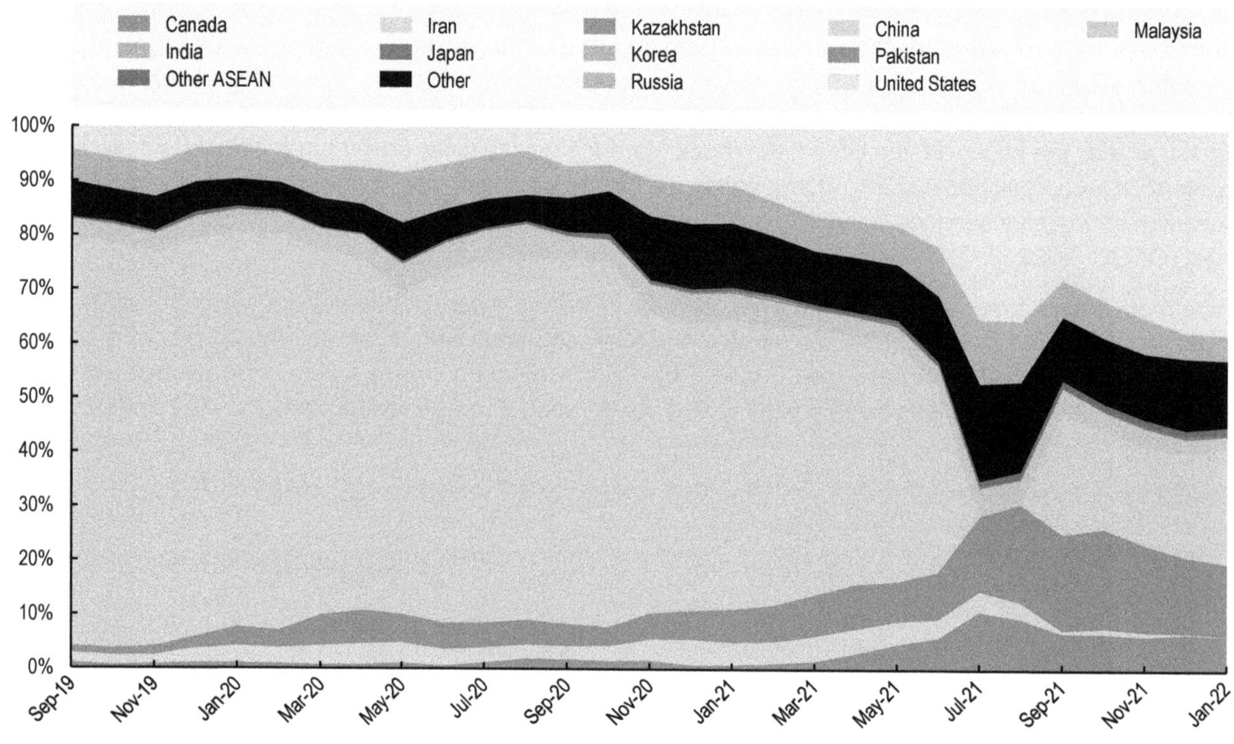

Source: Cambridge Bitcoin Electricity Consumption Index.

The People's Republic of China (hereafter 'China') has previously been dominating crypto-asset mining with more than half of total Bitcoin mining occurring in the country until January 2021, when crypto-asset trading and mining was banned over environmental concerns, given the heavy environmental footprint of this activity (OECD, 2022[14]). The ban led to relocation of mining activities to other parts of the world, such as the US and Kazakhstan, places that offered affordable energy sources. Although it could be presumed that part of the activity in Malaysia may have been supported by such relocations given geographical proximity, the increase in mining activity in Malaysia after the imposition of China's ban has been almost negligible. Additionally, it is estimated that miners in China moved towards masking their real locations in order to avoid being identified as operating in a country where restrictions apply (e.g. through IP VPN tools) (OECD, 2022[14]). Reasons related to energy supply, associated energy costs as well as local legislation may also partly contribute to such activity in ASEAN (Fortune.my, 2018[15]).

It should be highlighted, however, that there are important data gaps around crypto-asset mining activity that remain to be overcome. The importance of addressing such data challenge is high given the environmental impact of such activity and the need for robust and reliable data to support policy assessments and possible action (OECD, 2022[14]). It should also be noted that miners engage in activities that would be illegal in traditional markets such as front-running and sandwich trades, which leads to additional costs for retail investors (Auer, Frost and Vidal, 2022[16]).

Box 1.2. Crypto-asset mining and the negative environmental footprint of crypto-asset activity

The Bitcoin blockchain and other DLTs that validate transactions using proof-of-work consensus mechanisms (PoW) rely on the energy-intensive process of 'mining'.[1] Mining involves the use of aggregated computing power, and powerful computing hardware, to participate in the mechanism that determines what is recorded on a blockchain. As an incentive for consuming CPU time and electricity to support the network, mining participants are rewarded with new coins and transaction fees.

The use of energy-intensive transaction validation using PoW consensus mechanisms and the corresponding carbon footprint creates climate transition risks for participants in these markets. It can undermine the progress towards the climate transition and may not be correctly priced in, especially given the possible lack of awareness of such footprints by some of the holders and the lack of robust data about the measurement of such impact.

Given the carbon footprint and associated climate transition risks of certain digital assets, policy consideration and potential policy action is warranted. Outright banning of crypto-asset mining activity may not be the most effective solution to address these issues, given the risks of displacing or concealing such activity instead of curbing it, as was the case with the China ban of crypto-asset mining in 2021. This ban resulted in (a) the relocation of miners to other geographies with the same net effect for the globe; and (b) the concealing of activities still operating in China through the use of technical means.

In the absence of cross-border co-ordination, the negative externalities are being transferred from one geography to another, while the overall negative impact to the environment and societies remains the same.

1. In September 2022, the Ethereum blockchain on which the second largest crypto-asset (Ether or ETH) is based, transitioned from PoW to proof-of-stake (PoS) through a process known as 'the Merge', resulting in a 99% reduction of its environmental footprint.
Source: (OECD, 2022[14]).

1.3. Types of crypto-assets in ASEAN

Decentralised finance activity in ASEAN has been dominated by Bitcoin and stablecoins (Figure 1.7). In terms of unbacked crypto-assets, Ether is also heavily used, although to a lesser extent than Bitcoin. This follows global trends of preferences for these two mainstreamed crypto-assets, particularly when it comes to holdings by professional or institutional investors, either directly or through regulated products referencing Bitcoin (OECD, 2022[4]). As Bitcoin is the crypto-asset with the longest history and renown, it may inspire more investor confidence for having stood the test of time in the short life of crypto-markets. Both Bitcoin and Ether have gone through several cycles with deep bear markets, possibly creating the expectation by retail investors of continued patterns of cycle recovery.

Figure 1.7. Breakdown of crypto-asset activity in ASEAN by type of asset

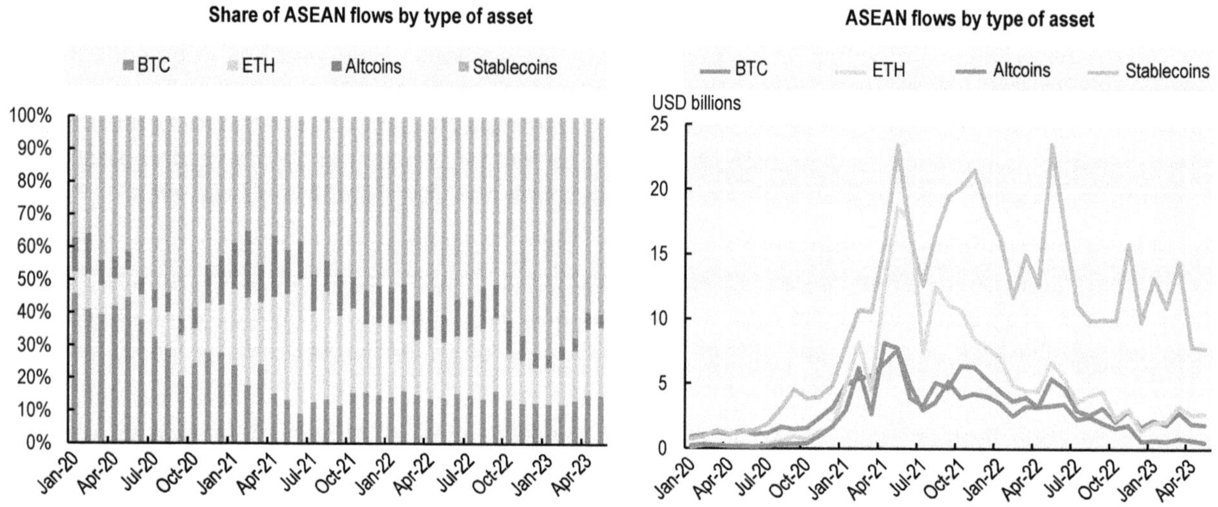

Note: includes Bitcoin, Ether, Altcoin crypto-assets and stablecoins. Stablecoins consist of BUSD, DAI, TUSD, USDC, USDP, USDT_BTC, USDT_ETH, USDT_TRX and Altcoin crypto-assets consist of DOGE, FTT, LTC, TRX, WBTC, WETH, XRP.
Source: OECD based on Chainalysis data.

1.4. The importance of stablecoins in the ASEAN ecosystem

The second largest category of assets in the ASEAN market is so-called stablecoins, which have historically constituted at least 50% of total flows in ASEAN throughout the period 2020-22 (Figure 1.7). Although initially designed by the industry to serve as a means of payment, with a stated ambition to be used widely by retail users to pay for goods and services and by corporations in the context of supply chain payments, stablecoins are used in their vast majority by crypto-asset investors. So-called stablecoins have been heavily used to facilitate trading, lending and borrowing and other transactions involving digital assets since the early days of development of crypto-asset markets. For example, stablecoins are used to move between crypto-assets or crypto-exchanges (e.g. lending, borrowing, collateral pledged on DeFi lending protocols, liquidity mining in DeFi), or to reduce their exposure to crypto-assets without having to convert their holdings to fiat and/or exit the decentralised finance space. Given that crypto-asset exchanges do not allow trading across all possible crypto-asset pairs, stablecoins' primary role has been that of a medium of exchange within these markets, similar to a euro-dollar instrument in non-US exchanges, and especially given their utility across different blockchains. Anecdotal evidence suggests that stablecoins in emerging market economies are also being used as a way to hedge against weak or volatile domestic currencies.

The proportion of stablecoins as a percentage of total ASEAN flows has increased significantly since the crypto winter in early 2022, which is in line with the global trend in the behaviour of crypto-asset investors wishing to protect themselves from the increased volatility of unbacked crypto-assets (e.g. Bitcoin). As such, investors have been shifting from unbacked crypto-assets towards stablecoins to reduce their exposure to the downturn, given the perception of relative stability of these instruments (that is, relative to unbacked crypto-assets). Stablecoins have therefore allowed crypto-asset holders to protect against mainstream crypto-asset volatility without having to exit the decentralised finance market or covert their holdings into fiat. Some crypto-asset holders could be intentionally avoiding the use of national currencies or traditional financial institutions to exit their investment in order to conceal illegal activity and/or evade taxation of earnings, among other reasons.

Figure 1.8. Claimed use cases of so-called stablecoin arrangements

MEANS OF PAYMENT FOR RETAIL TRANSACTIONS

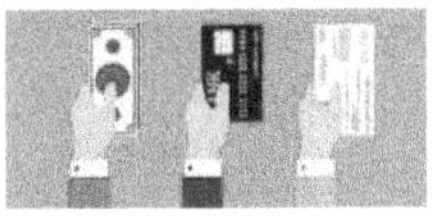

- Initial design and stated purpose to be used by retail users for payments
- Claim to address cross-border payment inefficiencies (e.g. international remittances)
- Today, estimated volume of stablecoins used for retail payments is **insignificant**

VEHICLE CURRENCY / MEDIUM OF EXCHANGE FOR CRYPTO-ASSET TRADING

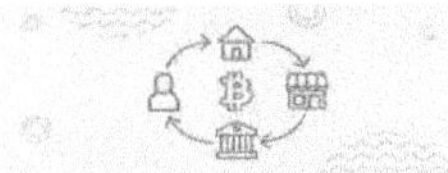

- **Facilitate trading** between crypto-asset pairs
- **Move** between crypto-assets or crypto-exchanges without having to convert to fiat

STORE OF VALUE

- **Hedge** / protect from highly volatile crypto-assets

KEY INGREDIENT OF DEFI

- Used as **collateral** in DeFi lending protocols; as trading facilitators in Decentralised Exchanges (DEXs) or for liquidity mining

Stablecoins are an indispensable ingredient and one of the foundations of DeFi protocols, and the increased DeFi activity in ASEAN may partly explain the increased proportion of stablecoins in overall crypto-asset activity in the region. They serve as collateral in lending protocols; are used to transfer funds from one protocol to another and are supplied to liquidity pools for swaps in Decentralised Exchanges (DEXs) and Automated Market Makers (AMMs) (OECD, 2022[4]). Also, as stablecoins are less volatile relative to other crypto-assets, holders of stablecoins may seek additional yields by investing in DeFi protocol activity, especially if they cannot exit these markets and convert to fiat – inter alia due to taxation constraints.

Figure 1.9. Cumulative stablecoin flows in ASEAN from 2020 to 2022

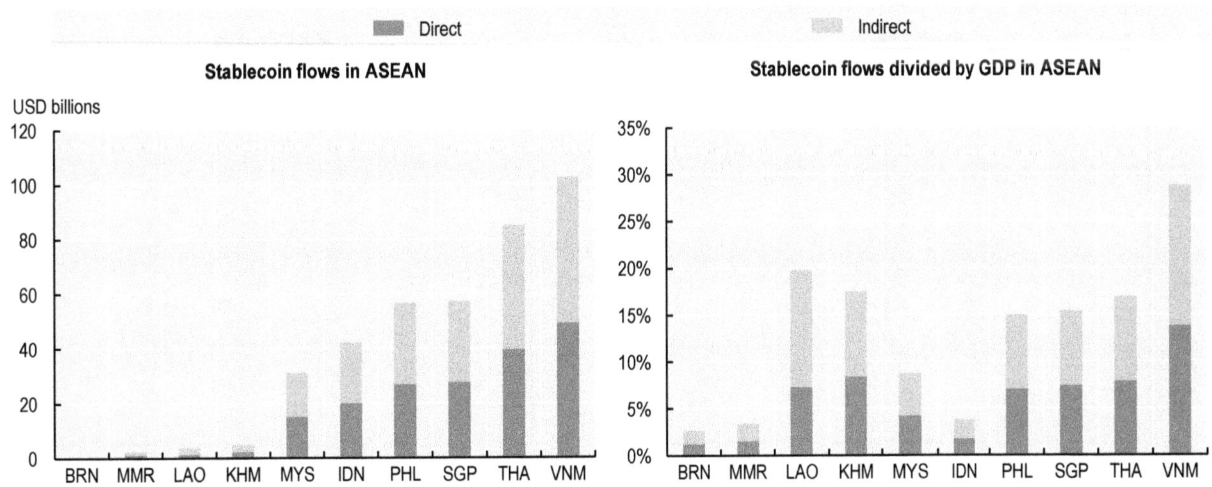

Note: Includes the following stablecoins: BUSD, DAI, TUSD, USDC, USDP, USDT_BTC, USDT_ETH, USDT_TRX. Based on average GDP for 2020 -2021 based on World Bank data. Direct flows are defined as a transfer of assets where the source and destination services are both counterparties to the transfer. Indirect flows denote a transfer of assets where at least one counterparty to the transfer is a self-hosted entity but where the ultimate source or destination of the transfer is described.
Source: OECD based on Chainalysis data.

1.5. DeFi protocol activity in Asia

DeFi protocol activity has been one of the fastest-growing[3] parts of the crypto-asset and wider decentralised finance ecosystem since the summer of 2020 (also known as the "DeFi summer"). Total value of crypto-assets locked in DeFi protocols on the Ethereum blockchain stood at 2.4bn in July 2020, and reached USD 108.8bn at the peak of the market in November 2021 (Figure 1.10). DeFi activity "tracks" the trend of mainstream crypto-assets given massive interconnectedness, dependencies and feedback loops between DeFi protocols and crypto-assets (OECD, 2022[3]).

Figure 1.10. DeFi and crypto-asset market evolution

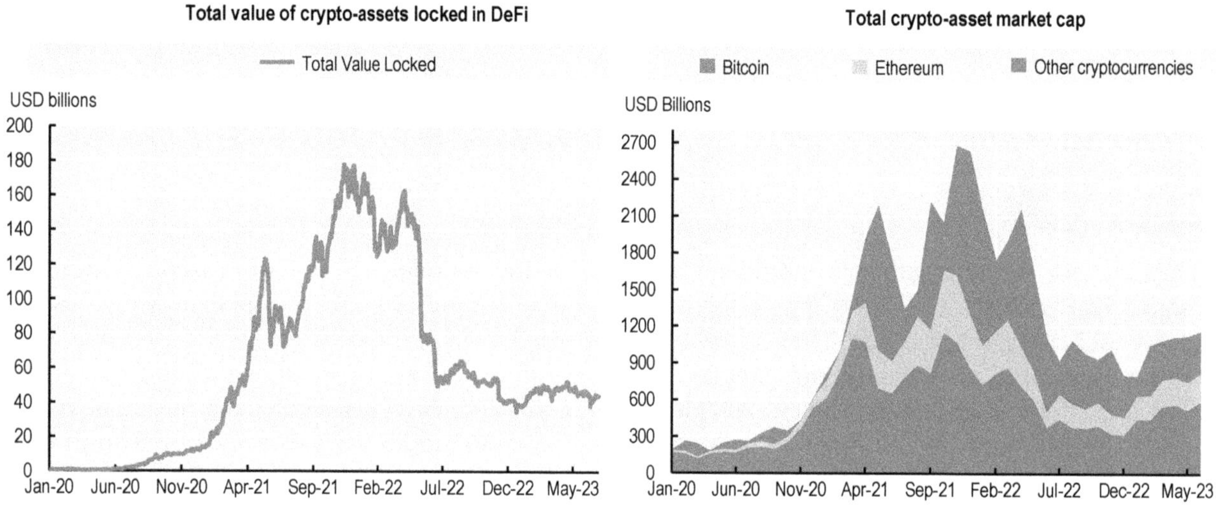

Source: DeFiLlama, from January 2020 to June 2023; Refinitive from January 2020 to June 2023.

Figure 1.11. DeFi ASEAN flows

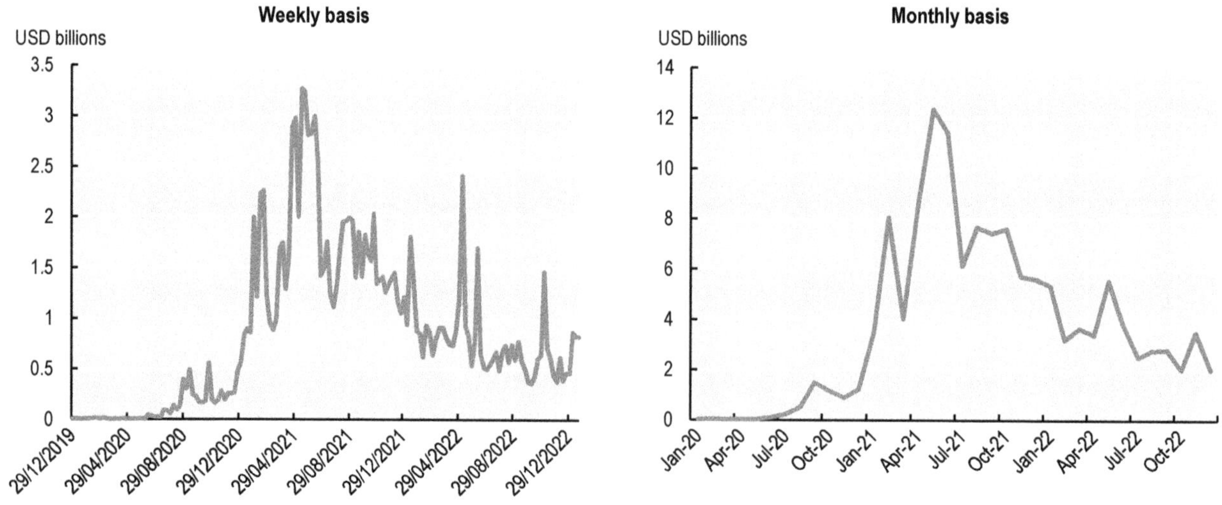

Source: OECD based on Chainalysis data.

DeFi protocol activity globally has been concentrated in DeFi lending and borrowing protocols and in decentralised exchanges (DEXs) and Automated Market Makers (AMMs) (OECD, 2022[2]). Activity in DeFi lending and borrowing protocols has been driven to a large extent by unrestricted leverage opportunities on the basis of crypto-assets. Crypto-assets are pledged as collateral in DeFi lending protocols in exchange for borrowed crypto-assets that can in turn be pledged as collateral on different protocols, building leverage in the system (OECD, 2022[4]). Most DeFi protocols have been historically built on the Ethereum blockchain given smart contract functionalities provided by the ERC-20 Token Standard. This could explain the important Ether flows towards DeFi globally and in ASEAN, too (Figure 1.12).

Figure 1.12. Inflows of Ether to DeFi by country in 2022

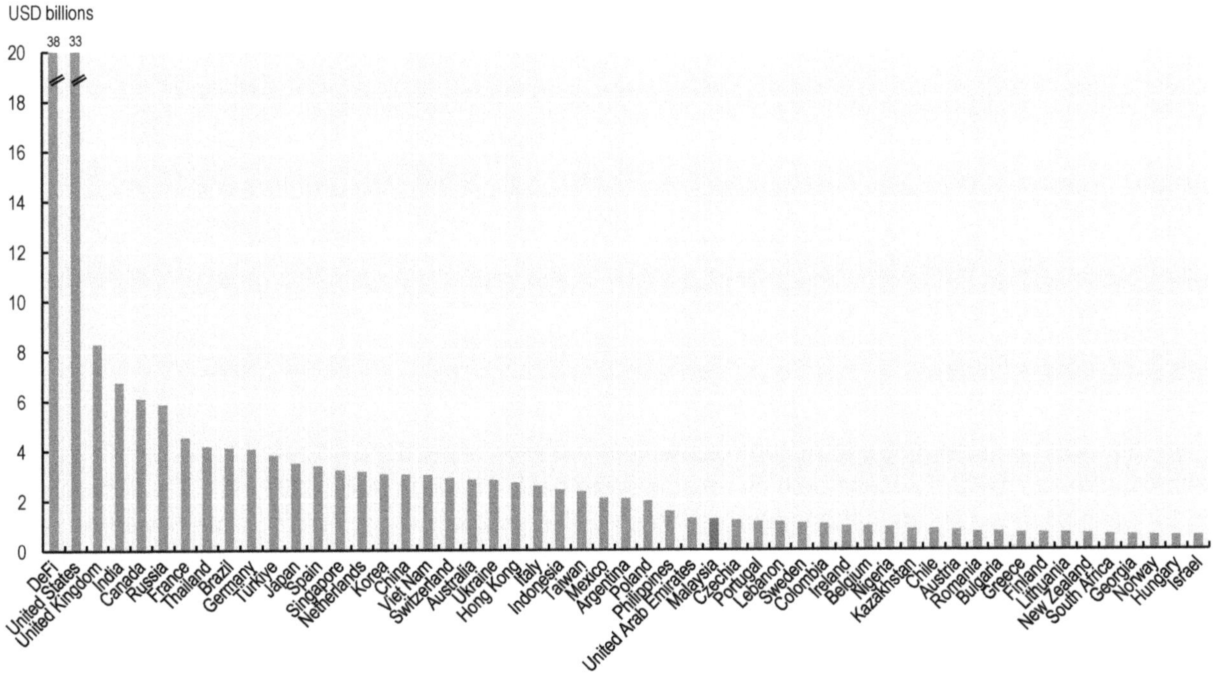

Source: OECD calculations based on Chainalysis data.

DEXs and AMMs[4] are disintermediated, peer-to-peer on-chain platforms where traders can swap crypto-assets for other crypto-assets - but not for fiat, as in most centralised crypto-exchanges.[5] Instead of order books, DEXs rely on liquidity pools where investors (liquidity providers) lock crypto-assets in exchange for rewards. Trading volumes in DEXs tend to follow the wider crypto-asset market volume trends, and particularly that of the Bitcoin, knowing that most crypto-asset prices tend to move in sync. Empirical evidence suggests that the most important crypto-assets are moderately positively correlated with each other over time, when daily and weekly returns are considered, and that the correlation strength increases significantly during downturns (Lahajnar and Rožanec, 2020[17]).

DEXs are an increasingly important part of the DeFi market, with growing market share as compared to centralised crypto-asset exchanges (CEXs), particularly following the recent failures of multi-function crypto-asset intermediaries and in spite of similar vulnerabilities around operational and cyber security risks. The vast majority of crypto-asset transaction activity had been happening at centralised exchanges for crypto-assets (CEXs) until early 2021, when DEX trading volumes started to become a meaningful part of the total activity, growing to almost 20% of the total trading activity as of H2 2022. Interestingly, DEXs have experienced a surge in trading volumes in the aftermath of the FTX failure, the Silicon Valley Bank and other major crises related to the crypto-asset market. This could be attributed to investors' lack of confidence and fear of losing access to their crypto-assets, given that DEXs involve self-custody of assets by the investors themselves without a third-party custodian.

Figure 1.13. Increasing part of crypto-asset trading occurring in DEXs

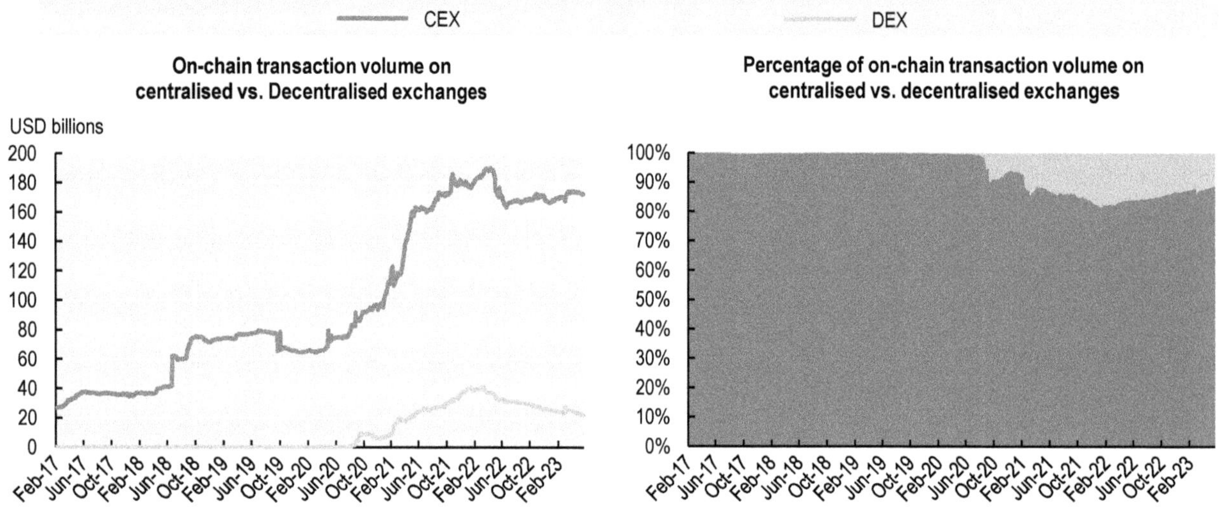

Note: CEX is defined as crypto-to-crypto exchanges and DEX is as decentralised exchanges
Source: OECD based on Chainalysis.

A depiction of estimated aggregate crypto-asset flows across continents indicates important flows from Asian countries to the DeFi space both on an aggregate basis for the period 2022 - H1 2023 (Figure 1.14) and for each of the years in that period (see Annex). This estimate, however, includes flows from large markets such as China, Japan and Korea. It should be noted that DeFi protocols have in most cases no defined jurisdiction and allow participation on a pseudonymous basis without KYC onboarding. It is therefore difficult to obtain accurate statistics of geographic breakdown of DeFi activity by geography.

Figure 1.14. Aggregate net flows across geographies from 2020 to 2023

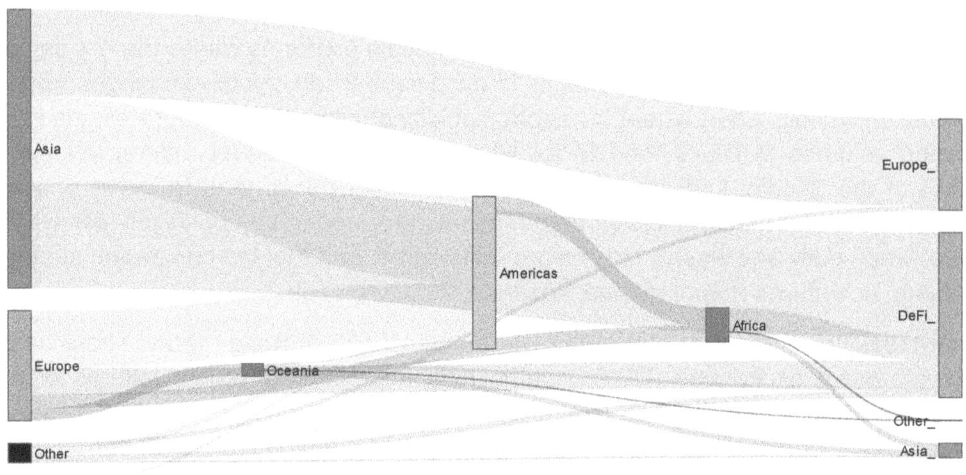

Note: Based on net flows measured in USD. DeFi represents smart contracts that facilitate financial intermediation of cryptocurrencies, for example lending or crowdfunding. Decentralised exchanges are included in the exchanges category.
Source: OECD based on Chainalysis data.

The prevailing crypto-assets in ASEAN are Bitcoin, Ether and the major so-called stablecoins USDT (Tether) and USDC (Circle), in line with the global trend of dominance of mainstream crypto-assets (Figure 1.15). The importance of Bitcoin flows in ASEAN has been decreasing over the years; Bitcoin flows constituted almost a third of all flows in 2020 and dropped to 15% of total as of 2022. Flows of Ether followed an opposite trend, accounting for 13.5% of total flows in 2020 and increasing to a third of total flows in 2021, and 20.0% of flows in 2022, perhaps driven also by the rise of DeFi protocols that were primarily based on the Ethereum.

USDT has been the prevailing so-called stablecoin used, accounting for a third of total flows to ASEAN, followed by USDC with 17% of total as of 2022. Stablecoins are issued on different chains, and in order to have a view on the usage of a particular stablecoin, the sum of the same stablecoin issued in different chains has to be considered (e.g. USDT issued on the Ethereum plus Tron blockchain are considered in this analysis). The pervasiveness of stablecoins is underlined by their multiple usage in crypto-asset systems (see Section 2 1.4).

Figure 1.15. Yearly Crypto-asset flows to ASEAN from 2022 to 2022

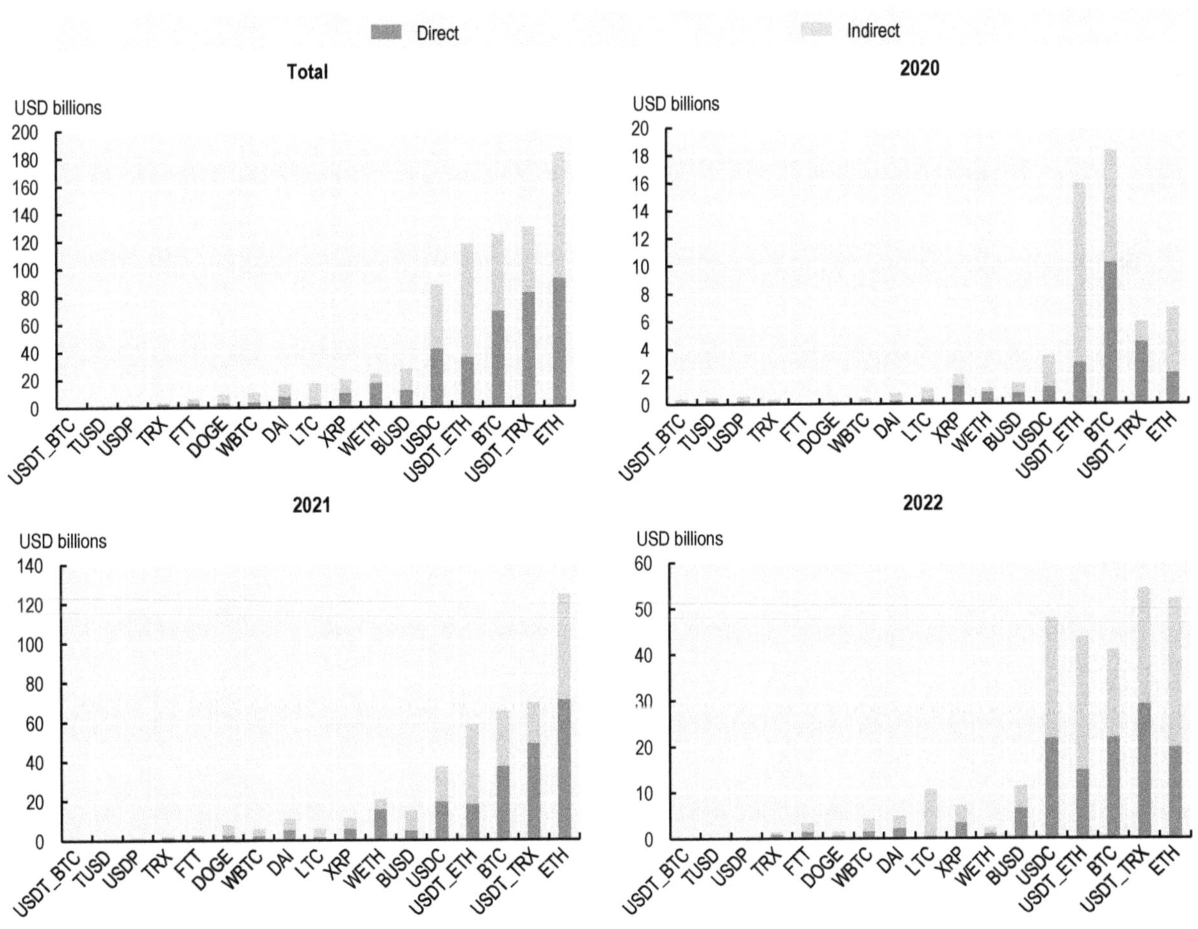

Note: Direct flows: a transfer of assets where the source and destination services are both counterparties to the transfer.
Indirect flows: a transfer of assets where at least one counterparty to the transfer is a self-hosted entity but where the ultimate source or destination of the transfer is described.
Assets: BTC, BUSD, DAI, DOGE, ETH, FTT, LTC, TRX, TUSD, USDC, USDP, USDT_BTC, USDT_ETH, USDT_TRX, WBTC, WETH, XRP.
Source: OECD based on Chainalysis data.

Notes

[1] AXS token market value reached USD 10bn at its peak and amounted to roughly USD 600 million as of December 2023.

[2] In some cases, the dependence of the value of such crypto-assets on the inflow of new clients was a characteristic shared with Ponzi schemes.

[3] And following the crypto-asset market downturn, one of the fastest-contracting parts of the wider decentralised finance market.

[4] e.g. Uniswap. AMMs are DEXs that pool liquidity from users and price the assets within a pool using algorithms. For the purposes of this report, DEX and AMM terms are used interchangeably.

[5] e.g. Coinbase.

2 The limits of DeFi for the democratisation of finance

Decentralised finance markets, including both DeFi protocols and crypto-assets (including stablecoins), have been marketed as a tool to promote financial inclusion. DeFi protocols claimed to constitute an alternative to traditional financial service provision that aims to democratise finance by replacing legacy, centralised institutions with peer-to-peer relationships that can provide a full spectrum of financial services, from everyday banking, loans and mortgages, to complicated contractual relationships and asset trading (Forbes Advisor, 2023[18]).

This chapter investigates the extent to which DeFi protocols, and crypto-asset markets more broadly, have delivered on their promise for the democratisation of finance and the promotion of financial inclusion. It finds that they have largely failed in this objective thus far and have instead exposed retail participants to disproportionately high risks. The chapter then examines alternative FinTech applications that could be better suited to promote financial inclusion in ASEAN and beyond, particularly for MSMEs.

2.1. Decentralised finance and the false promise of democratisation of finance

2.1.1. Professional investors dominating DeFi activity globally

Quantitative evidence suggests that professional and institutional investors have been the most active participants of decentralised finance markets. Using transaction sizes as a proxy, it can be inferred that more than 2/3 of global crypto-asset activity is performed by professional and/or institutional investors in every region analysed, and the share of professional activity as a part of total crypto-asset volume is the highest in East Asia (Figure 2.1).

Figure 2.1. Professional investors dominate decentralised finance activity in East Asia from July 2019 to June 2020

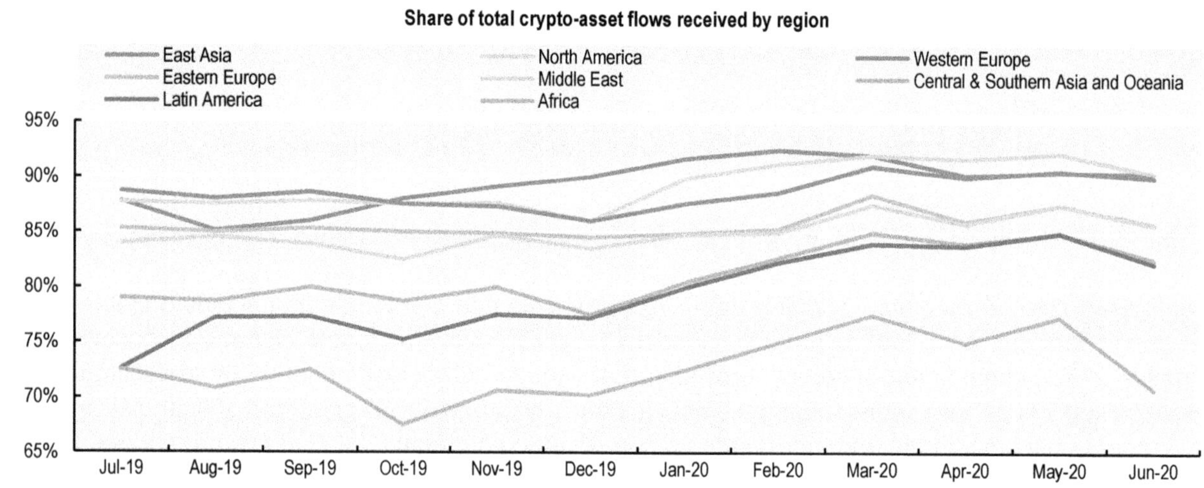

Source: OECD based on Chainalysis.

Such investors include large individual holders of crypto-assets (so-called 'crypto-whales'); centralised crypto-asset service providers, including exchanges (collectively known as "centralised finance" or CeFi); and institutional investors such as hedge funds or family offices. The latter are reported by industry sources to have been drawn into these markets by the opportunities for high returns, given that substantial volatility is one of the defining characteristics of mainstream crypto-assets.

When it comes to DeFi protocols in particular, retail participation has been almost negligible throughout the period 2020-2022 globally. Quantitative evidence around the DeFi protocols market suggests that large-sized transactions in DeFi, used as a proxy for institutional and professional investor participation, represented the largest share of DeFi activity throughout the short history of the DeFi market (Figure 2.2). Such investors could include hedge funds drawn into the DeFi protocol activity for the unrestricted leverage opportunities provided by DeFi lending and borrowing protocols, where crypto-assets can be posted as collateral to lever up multiple times (OECD, 2022[4]). This activity can also be explained by the prominent role of CeFi providers in the decentralised finance ecosystem. Such CeFi players (e.g. Celsius, FTX) performed multiple – and often conflicting – roles in the ecosystem and were heavily involved in DeFi protocol activity as this constituted means to secure some of the returns promised to their investors (OECD, 2022[3]).

Figure 2.2. Negligible minority of DeFi transactions come from retail investors from June 2020 to 31 January 2023

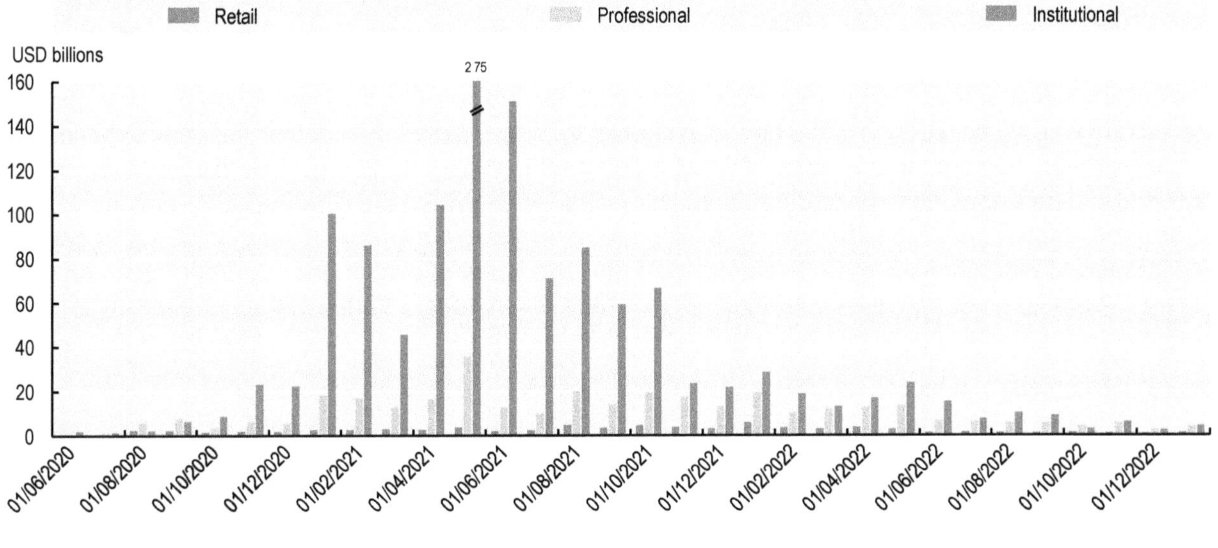

Note: Size of transaction as proxy. Institutional transactions representing those above USD 1 million, professional transactions representing those between USD 10K and USD 1 million, retail transactions representing those below USD 10K.
Source: OECD calculations based on Chainalysis data.

Interestingly, when looking into the inflows and outflows of funds to DeFi protocols, it can be observed that much of the flows coming into DeFi protocols are originating within the DeFi space itself (Figure 2.3). This points to the increased use of leverage within the decentralised finance system, with assets borrowed in DeFi borrowing and lending protocols re-used as collateral multiple times for further lending, for example. These flows could also be explained by the opportunistic shift from one platform to another given discrepancies in rates between platforms, or the shift to tokens and protocols depending on the yields offered at any point in time (OECD, 2022[4]).

Figure 2.3. Inflow of funds to DeFi by type of investor from June 1, 2020 to January 31, 2023

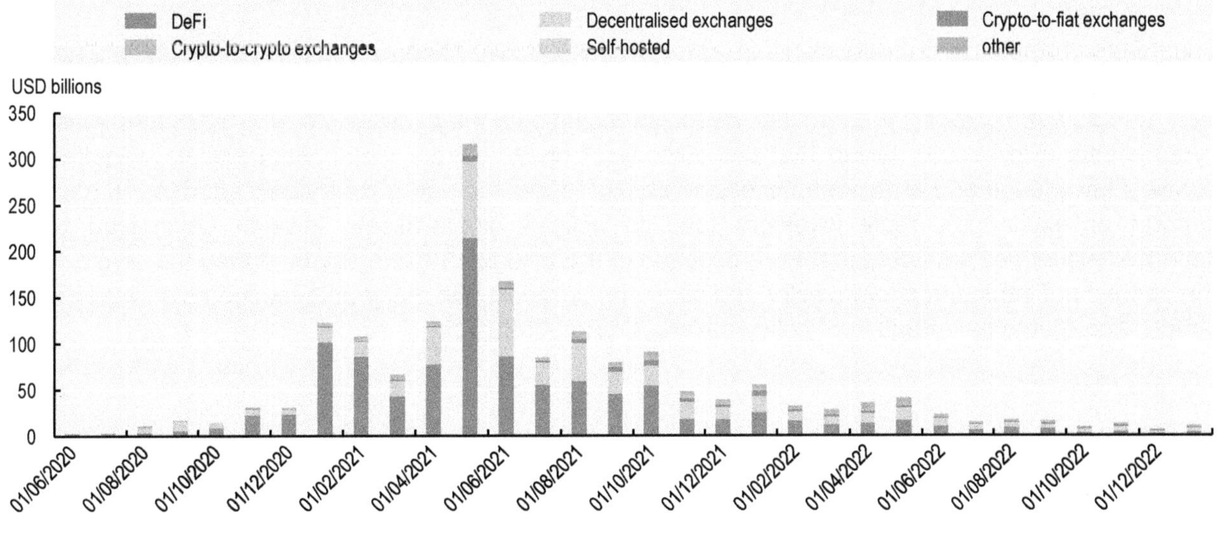

Note: DeFi category including DeFi protocols and excluding DEXs that are reported separately.
Source: OECD calculations based on Chainalysis data.

Trading behaviour across different types of exchanges also reveals a similar dominance of large professional market participants. The size of trades executed at centralised exchanges (CEXs) and decentralised exchanges (DEXs) indicate that participation in DeFi is dominated by large-size trades, most akin to activity from professional investors, including so-called 'whales', rather than small retail players (Figure 2.4). The average trade size on DEXs, particularly in the case of stablecoin trading, is ten to one hundred times higher than the average trade size on CEXs. Indicatively, the highest weekly average trade size for Uniswap V2 was USD 14 000 and for Uniswap V3 was USD 95 000, compared against centralised exchanges with average trade sizes of USD 1 000-4 000 (Carey, 2023[19]). This discrepancy can be attributed to differences in the price determination mechanism between the different DEXs and the different capacity of AMMs to absorb large trades resulting to relatively low slippage (Carey, 2023[19]). It can also be attributed to differences in the microstructure of the two types of exchanges, as order books on CEXs split trades based on order size, while liquidity pools on DEXs execute trades in their original size.

Figure 2.4. Average trade size in DEXs vs. CEXsof March 1, 2023 – July 22, 2023

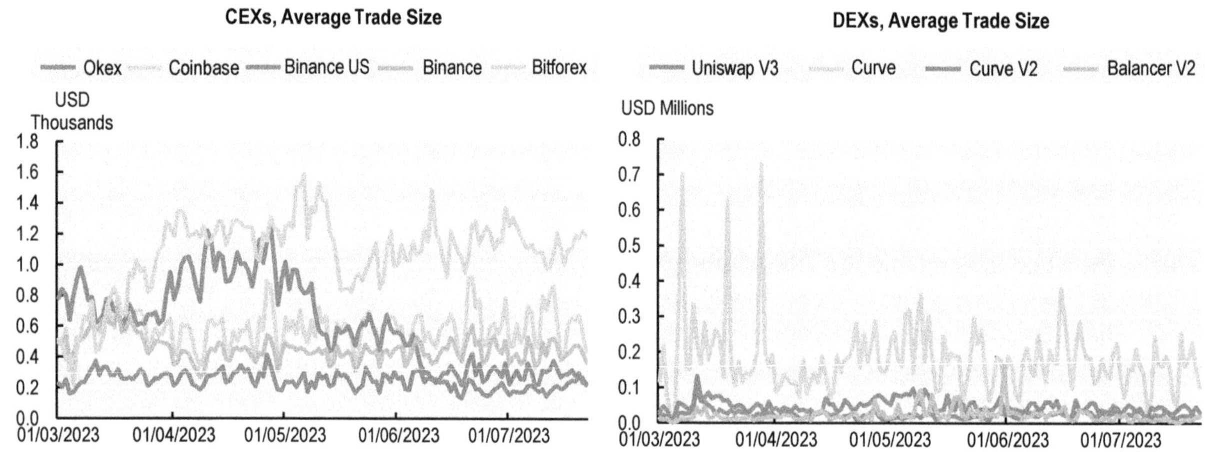

Source: Kaiko.

2.1.2. Retail investors disproportionately affected by the crypto winter

Despite the prominence of professional investors in decentralised finance markets, there are still sizeable amounts of retail users participating in these markets. In fact, the number of small wallet holders, which is used here as a proxy for retail users, has been increasing over the period 2020 – H1 2023 for mainstream crypto-assets (Figure 2.5). Given that self-custody of crypto-assets (self-hosted wallets) require more technical knowledge and skills than accessing crypto-assets through a centralised interface (e.g. trading platform or exchange), retail investors tend to access crypto-assets through centralised trading platforms/exchanges and were therefore exposed to the failures of CeFi players during the crypto winter. The absence of safeguards for investor and consumer protection in many of these markets, retail investor participation merits the attention of policymakers (OECD, 2022[3]).

Figure 2.5. Number of retail holders of mainstream crypto-assets and stablecoins from 2020 to H1 2023

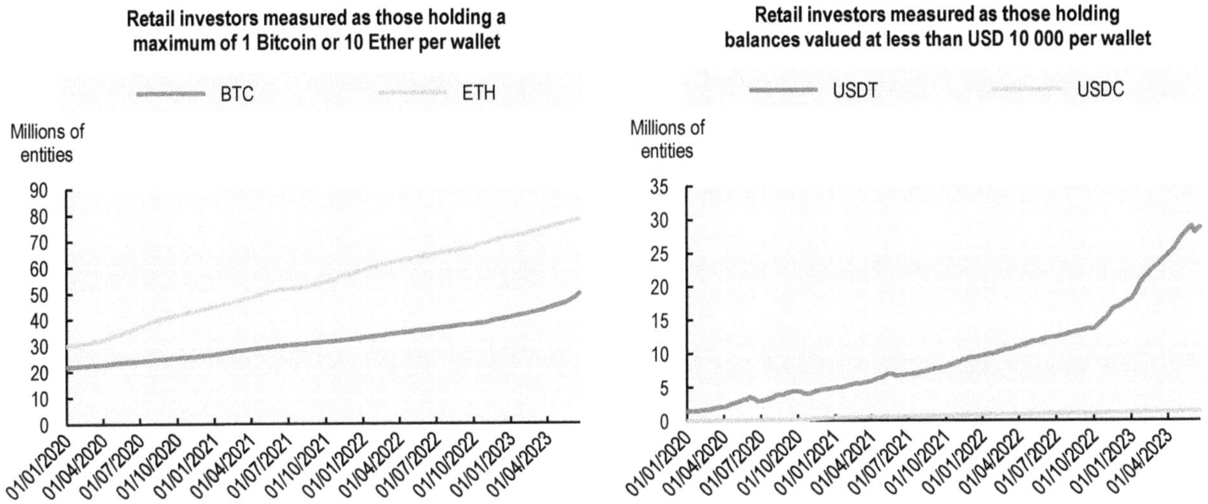

Note: Retail holders considered as holders with maximum 1 Bitcoin or 10 Ether tokens in their wallet, respectively (LHS) and that have a balance of up to USD 10 000 equivalent of USDC or USDT (RHS).
Source: OECD calculations based on Chainalysis data.

The 2022-23 crypto-asset market downturn has left retail investors particularly exposed to important losses without any recourse. The impact of the crypto-asset failures on many retail crypto-asset market participants has been disproportionately high compared to large crypto-asset investors or dominant market participants who appeared to close positions with limited losses or even a profit. Indicatively, in the case of the Terra Luna collapse, several large investors appeared to have exited their positions in UST much earlier than many smaller investors, while some small investors also continued buying during the collapse (Shah and Latif, 2022[20]; Bloomberg, 2022[21]). In line with this trend, analysis of transaction data on Bitcoin trades show evidence of smaller Bitcoin wallets being net buyers during the crypto-asset market downturn, against large wallets that offloaded their Bitcoin holdings in the aftermath of the failures (OECD, 2022[4]) (Figure 2.6). Empirical studies based on data on major crypto trading platforms over August 2015 – December 2022 show that a majority of crypto app users in nearly all economies made losses on their bitcoin holdings (Cornelli et al., 2023[22]).

Figure 2.6. Small Bitcoin holders net buyers during the crypto winter, large holders sellers as of end September 2022

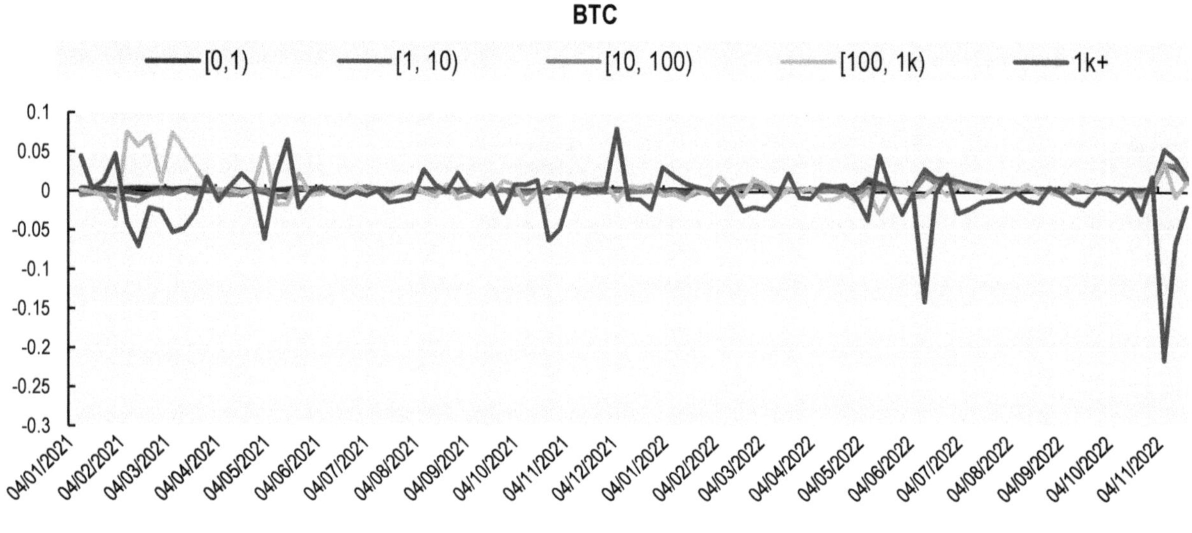

Note: Change in holdings of Bitcoin for a size category, expressed in millions of crypto-assets held by the entity at the last week for each month.
Source: (OECD, 2022[4]).

2.1.3. Complexity and non-custodial nature of DeFi make them unsuitable for underbanked/underserviced parts of the population

In addition to involving unregulated or uncompliant financial service provision, the complexity of DeFi protocols and their non-custodial nature make these practically difficult, if not outright unsuitable, for retail participants and therefore unfitting for financial inclusion purposes. For a non-programmer, it is difficult to interact with the interfaces of DeFi protocols if one is not familiar with blockchain technology and has no coding skills, given the technical complexity of DLTs and composable DeFi applications (OECD, 2022[2]). Even with the emergence of more user-friendly interfaces, most aspects of current DeFi activity are difficult to grasp for the average retail participant in need of access to basic financial services. Complex strategies of leveraged trading and rehypothecation of crypto-assets are the prevailing activities in DeFi today, which clearly cannot lend themselves to objectives such as the promotion of access to basic financial services. For their most part, these do not involve any real assets or financing of real projects, thus making them unfit for real economy financing purposes. When it comes to DeFi lending protocols in particular, due to the anonymity of borrowers, over-collateralisation is pervasive, and reliance on collateral limits access to credit to borrowers who are already asset-rich, negating financial inclusion benefits (Aramonte et al., 2022[23]).

The non-custodial nature of DeFi is one of its main defining characteristics that could be unfitting for the average retail investor. Users hold exclusive control over their private keys, and thus, their own assets (until they transact) without assistance from intermediaries such as traditional regulated custodians (OECD, 2022[2]). This means that users are exposed to increased risk of losing their assets, as the loss of private keys translates into loss of access to their investment. Indeed, the loss of a user's private key is one of the most common risks facing inexperienced users and translates into loss of access to all assets associated with the private key, as decentralised spaces do not allow for forced transfer mechanisms (OECD, 2020[24]). The use of non-custodial or un-hosted wallets as the means to access the DeFi ecosystem at this stage of development of the market adds an extra layer of complexity and risk that are once again unfit for the uninitiated and non-tech savvy average retail user. It should also be noted that retail investors are therefore most likely to invest in DeFi protocol activity through centralised intermediaries, as has been the example through staking products offered to them by centralised entities.

2.1.4. Speculative forces driving crypto-asset activity rather than real use-cases: short-termism and the case of stablecoins

Crypto-asset activity has been driven to a large extent by speculation and fear of missing out, particularly during the prolonged period of ultra-low interest rates. Previous OECD analysis has shown that other motives, such as the use of crypto-assets for portfolio diversification or as an inflation hedge, do not hold (OECD, 2022[4]). Based on surveys, the upside potential for yield in crypto-assets appears to have attracted the interest of investors (private and professional alike) as a vehicle for speculation given the potential for outsized returns.

Several additional arguments can further substantiate the conclusion that crypto-asset use is a speculative instrument rather than a tool with real practical use cases, such as payments. The difficulty in valuing crypto-assets and the huge volatility of these assets make them unsuitable for payments purposes. When looking at trading data classified by duration of holding prior to the trade, holders of less than two weeks have historically the lion's share of total flows, followed by exchanges (Figure 2.7). This may indicate short-termism in trading activity of crypto-asset holders and speculative investment behaviour.

Figure 2.7. Total crypto-asset flows by time horizon profile

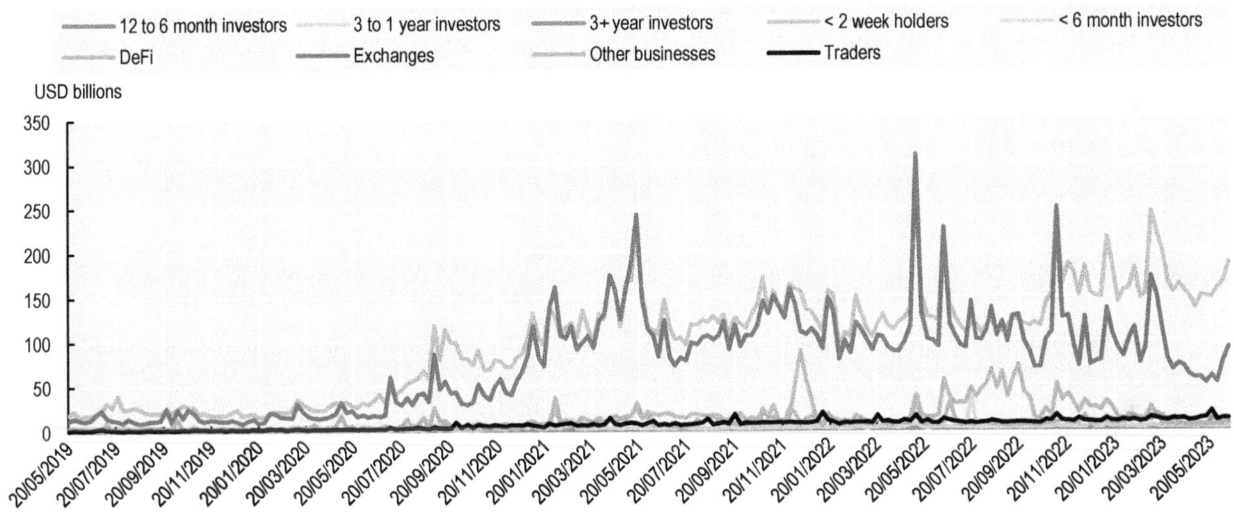

Note: Flows a weekly basis.
Source: OECD calculations based on Chainalysis data.

When it comes to stablecoins, one of the possible uses of such instruments is for payments and international remittances (see Section 1.4). In Europe, surveys of crypto-asset owners have indicated that these are hardly ever used for payments (ECB, 2022[25]). The extent to which many existing unregulated stablecoins are being used for these purposes in ASEAN and beyond is difficult to assess, although there are some indications that stablecoins are currently being used mostly for cases other than remittances. Stablecoins, and in particular USDC and DAI, have been extensively used in DeFi protocols as collateral in lending and borrowing (Figure 2.8). Unregulated stablecoins give rise to multiple risks for users and for markets overall, including unreliable reserves and unclear redemption rights for holders, making them unsuited for safe remittance use cases.

Figure 2.8. Stablecoin usage in DeFi activity one of the major current use cases globally

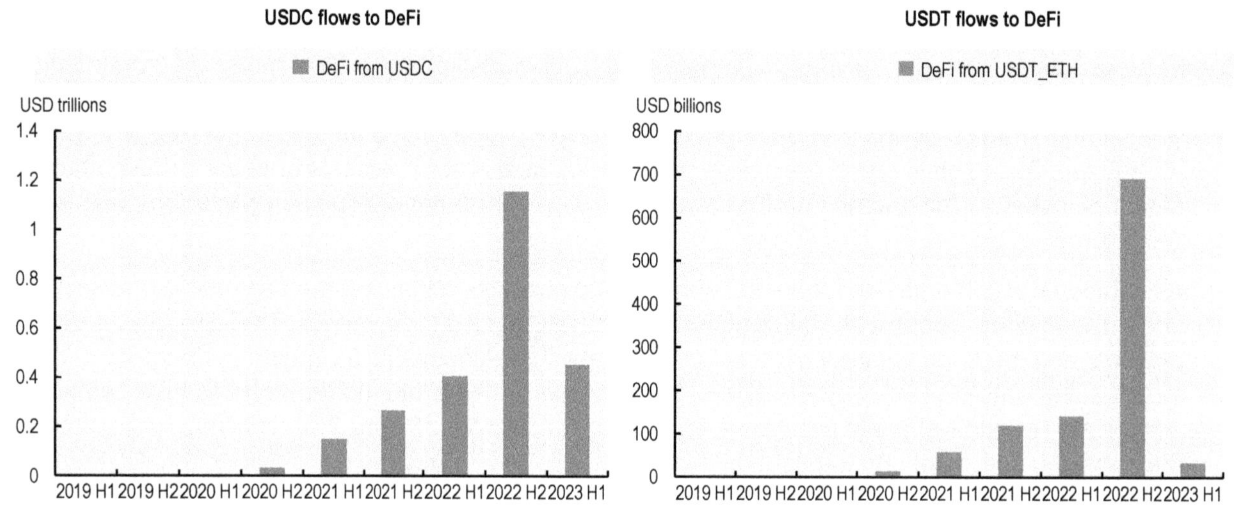

Source: OECD Calculations based on Chainalysis data.

Data on USDC usage in DeFi are indicative of the heavy use of stablecoins in DeFi markets, particularly from professional investors. The majority of USDC trading happens in DEXs (Figure 2.9), and it is estimated that in 2022, DeFi lending protocols MakerDAO, Compound and Aave held on average about 10.5% of the total USDC supply (Figure 2.10).

Figure 2.9. USDC trading volume on DEXs vs. CEXs

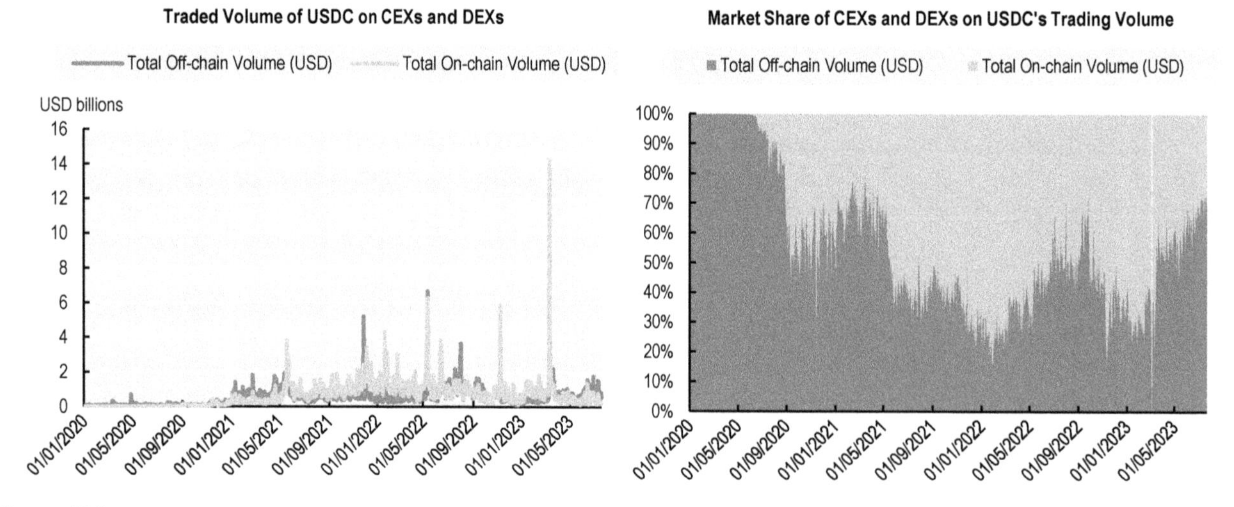

Source: Kaiko.

Figure 2.10. USDC liquidity deposited on ETH-based DeFi lending protocols

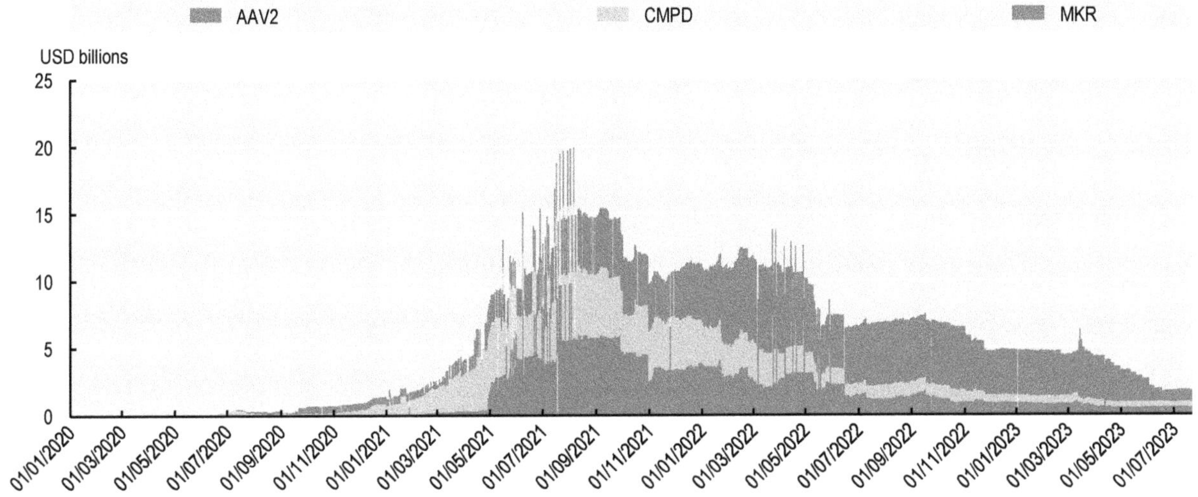

Source: Kaiko.

The high correlation between stablecoin and altcoin (unbacked crypto-assets beyond the mainstream bitcoin and ether) flows in ASEAN could underline the increased use of stablecoins as a medium of exchange within crypto-asset markets, rather than for international remittance use cases (Figure 2.11). Indeed, crypto-asset exchanges do not allow trading across all possible crypto-asset pairs, and trading of small altcoins need to go through a stablecoin first. Similarly, stablecoins can be used to transfer funds from one chain to another, given their existence in multiple chains ('multi-chain' stablecoins).

Figure 2.11. Correlation between Stablecoin and Altcoin in ASEAN from 2020 to 2022

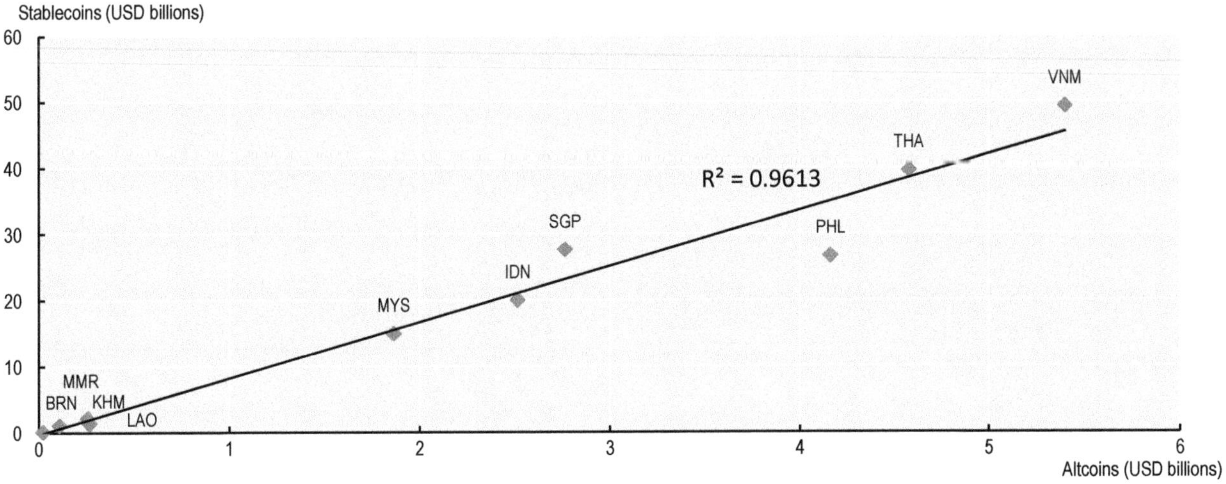

Note: Assets included: BUSD, DAI, DOGE, FTT, LTC, TRX, TUSD, USDC, USDP, USDT_BTC, USDT_ETH, USDT_TRX, XRP
Source: OECD calculations based on Chainalysis data.

It should also be noted that currently, the stablecoin market is a highly concentrated market, both at the issuance and at the holding level. At the issuance level, the top two stablecoins account for 87% of the total market (as of 4 July 2023) (Figure 2.12). At the holder level, investors account for a quarter and close to one half of total stablecoins available for the top two stablecoins, USDT and USDC respectively (Figure 2.13).

Figure 2.12. Stablecoin market breakdown from July 2020 to July 2023

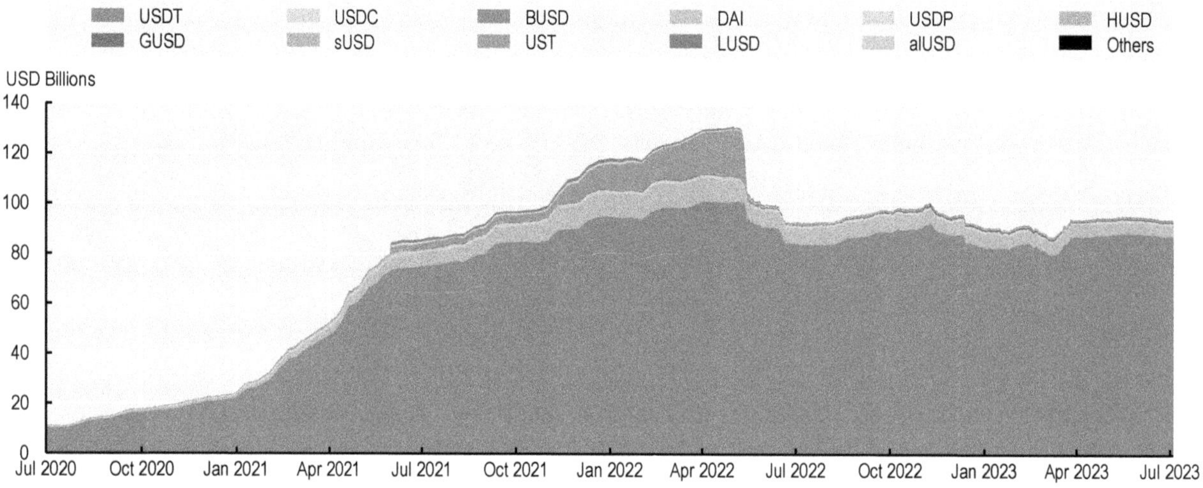

Source: OECD calculations based on CoinMarketCap and CoinMetrics data.

Figure 2.13. Stablecoins holding distribution by type of holder

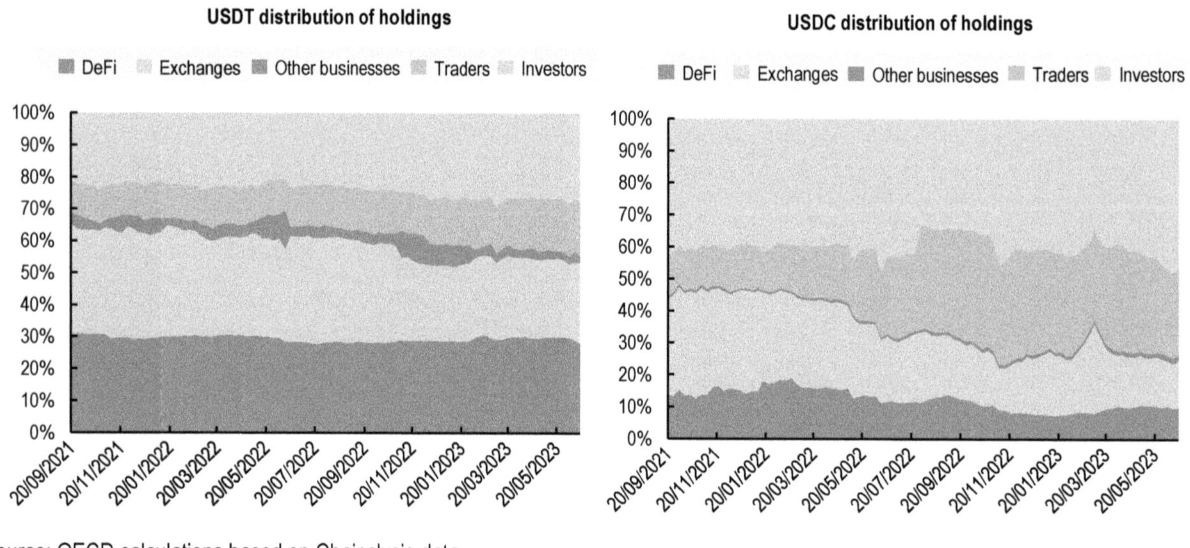

Source: OECD calculations based on Chainalysis data.

Many retail investors driven into decentralised finance markets by speculative motives may not be sufficiently aware of the risks related to such investments, and this is why policy consideration and action is warranted. Consistent policy frameworks around decentralised finance, coupled by a better understanding of the risks involved by investors, should be fostered. In parallel, there is merit in considering promoting other FinTech applications with possible beneficial impacts on financial inclusion, some examples of which are provided in Section 3.

3 FinTech applications with potential benefits for financial inclusion

ASEAN is the fastest growing internet market in the world, with an estimated 125 000 new internet users every day (WEF, 2023[26]), while the wider Asian region is home to an increasingly urban, literate, and young population that is keen to adopt new technologies across sectors, including in finance (OECD, 2021[27]). This provides fertile ground for FinTech applications to fill in some gaps in the provision of financial services to underserved parts of the region.

Indeed, the increased usage of digital finance applications during the COVID-19 pandemic (Fu and Mishra, 2020[28]) has been a great example of the possible benefits of FinTech applications for financial inclusion. According to the CCAF ASEAN FinTech benchmarking study, FinTechs in the region tend to cater to traditionally excluded populations in line with the Global Findex rankings of the respective countries (Figure 3.1). Although FinTech customers in ASEAN are more likely to be already banked individuals, important part of FinTech adopters are underbanked or unbanked individuals. In parallel, investment is flowing into FinTech development, with ASEAN's share of global FinTech funding standing at 7% in 2021, up from 2% in 2018, although Singapore and Indonesia account for more than two thirds of this funding (UOB, PWC and Association, 2022[29]).

This chapter discusses some examples of use cases that could be conducive to better servicing underbanked parts of the population, such as MSMEs or populations in rural parts of the region and provides some examples of practical applications from the ASEAN region.

Figure 3.1. Underserved part of ASEAN population and banked status of FinTech customers

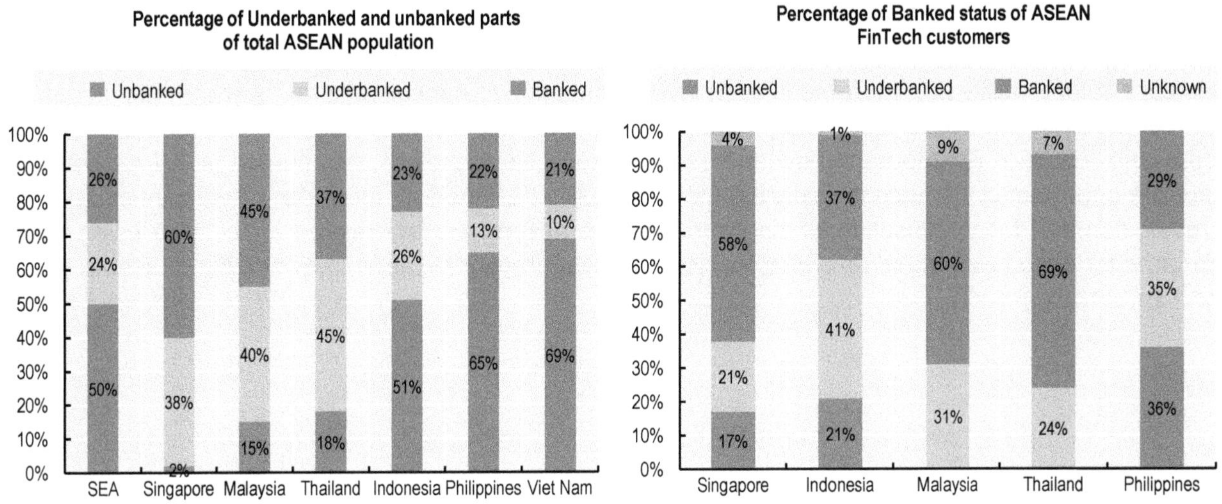

Source: Euromonitor, World Bank, Bain and Temasek, CCAF.

3.1. Regulated DLT-based finance: tokenisation and regulated digital assets

Although decentralised finance markets at their current stage expose investors to significant risks, concepts derived by DeFi protocols and regulated/compliant digital assets could potentially become a relevant part of the financial system at the institutional (i.e. non-retail) level in the future. Technologies and mechanisms associated with decentralised finance that may need to be further explored could potentially produce efficiencies and drive productivity gains in financial markets by improving the effectiveness and safety of trading and settlement at the infrastructure level (OECD, 2020[24]). These include atomic or programmable settlement of securities and payments at the post-trade, with the possibility for seamless delivery versus payment (DvP) or payment versus payment (PvP), increased automation and corresponding efficiency gains and enhanced transparency, as well as increased use of automation and programmability as is the case with smart contracts functionalities.

Policymakers are considering ways to allow for safe and responsible innovation, anticipating and addressing emerging risks for participants and markets. Technical level experimentation is already taking place with innovative pilots involving public-private co-operation, with the participation of traditional and decentralised finance entities. Project Mariana, for example, is a proof of concept launched by the Bank of International Settlements (BIS) Innovation Hub together with the Banque de France, Monetary Authority of Singapore and Swiss National Bank in co-operation with DeFi protocols, and explores the use of Automated Market Makers (AMMs) such as those deployed by DEXs in foreign exchange markets using CBDCs (BIS Innovation Hubs, 2023[30]). Project Guardian is a collaborative initiative led by the Monetary Authority of Singapore and with the participation of other regulators such as the Financial Services Agency of Japan, which seeks to test the feasibility of applications in asset tokenisation and DeFi while managing risks to financial stability and integrity (MAS, 2022[31]; FSA, 2023[32]).

The tokenisation of assets is indeed one of the most promising applications of DLTs in finance with numerous potential benefits (OECD, 2020[24]). It involves the digital representation of rights to real assets on distributed ledgers, or the issuance of traditional asset classes in tokenised form. Potential benefits include efficiency gains driven by automation and disintermediation; transparency; improved liquidity potential and tradability of assets which currently have near-absent liquidity; and faster and potentially more efficient clearing and settlement. When it comes to the impact on retail investors, tokenisation offers an additional tool for fractional ownership of assets[1] allowing for small minimum investments, which, in turn, could lower barriers to investment and promote more inclusive access to previously unaffordable or insufficiently divisive asset classes, such as real estate (see Box 3).

The example of tokenisation of real estate assets is a noteworthy one given that retail investors are usually restricted in their ability to participate in such investments due to capital constraints and limited access to commercial projects. Some real estate tokenisation platforms have emerged in Asia, such as KASA in Korea and ADDX in Singapore (Chow and Tan, 2022[33]). Nevertheless, this market is still nascent and there are important challenges to real estate tokenisation which include, inter alia, insufficient evidence of investor demand for tokenisation of single real estate assets and the related difficulty in using digital platforms for such investment, as well rules governing the fractionalisation of ownership of assets (Chow and Tan, 2022[33]).

Box 3.1. Real estate tokenisation: The example of Thailand

The first regulated asset-backed tokenisation backed by real estate in Thailand took place in 2021, with the issuance of SiriHub Token by SPV77 Co. Ltd., a Special Purpose Vehicle (SPV) set up to issue and offer the tokens. The offering consisted of a commercial real estate asset (Siri Campus Office Building valued at THB 2.4 billion, or USD 73 million) as the underlying asset, which was under a long-term lease commitment of 12 years to a single tenant at the time of the offering. The issuer filed a white paper with the Thai Securities and Exchange Commission (SEC) and complied with the SEC's requirements for initial coin offerings (Emergency Decree on the Amendment of the Revenue Code No. 19 B.E. 2561 A.D. 2018) (Okanurak and Koohasaneh, 2018[34]).

The token was designed for a term of four years and tokenholders were entitled to revenues from both the rentals and the potential sale of the asset through an auction at the end of the term. The SiriHub Token was offered in two tranches to cater for investors with different risk appetite. The minimum investment ticket for this offering was THB 10 (about USD 0.30) and 240 million tokens have been issued. Subscription for the tokens was via an online app (XSpring) available 24/7. The SiriHub Token was approved by the SEC and began trading at the digital exchange managed by ERX Company Limited in October 2021 (Chow and Tan, 2022[33]). Also in 2021, the Thai SEC granted a license to Fraction, a wholly owned subsidiary of Hong Kong based FinTech company Fraction Group, to host and trade tokens for fractional ownership of physical or digital assets.

The possible benefits of the transaction include fractionalisation and the possibility for retail investors to participate in a commercial real estate investment with as little as THB 10, potential economic efficiencies and possibilities customisation of the transaction. Thailand's real estate-backed tokenisation offering is conceptually similar to a real estate investment trust, with a passive trust mechanism whereby the SPV acts as the trustee holding the title deed of the property on behalf of the unit holders of the trust, and has to be a legal entity that ensures the underlying asset is not transferred, disposed of or encumbered without the tokenholders' approval.

In addition, and in order to prevent asset bubbles from being created by a possible future increased use of such offerings, a 2021 amendment specified that the real estate to be tokenised must not be a single condo unit or house and must constitute more than 80% in number or investment value of the project or in aggregate of not less than THB 500 million (USD 16.4 million) in order to be eligible for tokenisation (Securities Exchange Commission, 2020[35]).

Figure 3.2. SiriHub real estate tokenisation transaction structure

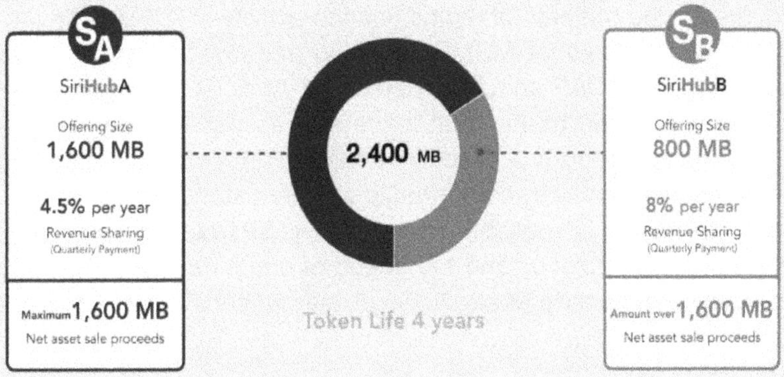

Source: Public information (https://spv77.digital/?lang=en).

The flow of private financing from capital owners to SMEs could also be eased and facilitated through regulated Security Token Offerings (STOs). Indeed, several countries in ASEAN have opted for tailor-made regulatory frameworks for STOs in addition to Thailand, including Malaysia, the Philippines (proposal stage) and Singapore (see Box 3.2) (OECD, 2020[36]). Frameworks for STOs have also been implemented in Asia beyond ASEAN, with the most prominent examples being that of Korea (FSC, 2023[37]) and Japan (FSA, 2019[38]). These frameworks all require issuers and intermediaries of such regulated tokenised security offerings to comply with securities regulations in respective jurisdictions, given the technology neutral approach to regulation. Tailor-made frameworks and guidance may promote legal certainty and assist market participants in understanding the requirements, equipping them to participate in such endeavours in a compliant and safe manner.

Box 3.2. Singapore framework for digital token offerings

Singapore clarified its regulatory position around the offering of digital tokens as early as 2017, and has issued a detailed guide to digital token offerings a year later (Monetary Authority of Singapore, 2017[39]; Monetary Authority of Singapore, 2020[40]).

According to the Singapore framework, digital tokens may represent ownership or a security interest over an issuer's assets or property and the Monetary Authority of Singapore (MAS) will examine the structure and characteristics of, including the rights attached to, a digital token in determining if the digital token is a type of capital markets product under the Securities and Futures Act (SFA). Digital tokens may also represent a debt owed by an issuer and be considered a debenture under the SFA, or a securities-based derivatives contract in case any derivatives are included.

Where digital tokens fall within the definition of securities, issuers of such tokens would be required to lodge and register a prospectus with MAS prior to the offer of such tokens, unless exempted based on proportionality (offering size lower than SGD 3 million and offer made to less than 50 investors in any period of 12 months, or offer made to accredited and institutional investors). Issuers and intermediaries are all subject to licensing requirements, while platforms facilitating secondary trading of such tokens would also have to be approved or recognised by MAS as an approved exchange or recognised market operator respectively under the SFA.

Source: Monetary Authority of Singapore.

3.1.1. *FinTech lending and the use of artificial intelligence for credit scoring*

FinTech lending accounts for the majority of digital finance activity in ASEAN driven by strong growth in consumer spending, increased needs for MSME financing and low banking penetration (as of 2019, in number of FinTech companies) (CCAF and ADBI, 2019[41]). Artificial intelligence (AI)-based models and big data are increasingly being used by FinTech lenders to assess the creditworthiness of prospective borrowers and make underwriting decisions. Machine Learning (ML) models are used to predict borrowers' defaults with superior forecasting accuracy compared to standard statistical models (e.g. logic regressions) especially when limited information is available (Bank of Italy, 2019[42]; Albanesi and Vamossy, 2019[43]). They can also improve both the efficiency and the speed of credit decision making and improve the risk prediction accuracy overall (Gambacorta et al., 2019[44]), although their use comes with a number of risks and challenges.

The use of AI-based models for credit scoring could have potential beneficial impacts on the extension of credit to MSMEs, both through a reduction in the cost of underwriting, and through improvements in the analysis of creditworthiness of clients with limited credit history and/or without collateral ('thin files') (OECD,

2021[45]). It can therefore enable the extension of credit to young start-ups and MSMEs that cannot prove their viability through historical performance data or tangible collateral assets, potentially enhancing access to credit and supporting the growth of the real economy by alleviating constraints to MSME financing.

Although there are many potential gains from AI in terms of cost reduction and financial inclusion, there are also risks stemming from its use. Risks involve data quality and confidentiality, limited explainability of the models used and possible risks to financial consumers (OECD, 2021[45]). In particular, the use of credit rating models based on such techniques can raise risks of disparate impact in credit outcomes and the potential for discriminatory or unfair lending (US Treasury, 2016[46]). Well-intentioned ML models may inadvertently generate biased conclusions, discriminate against certain classes of people (e.g. based on race, gender, ethnicity, religion), or simply reinforce existing biases, while making discrimination in credit allocation more difficult to identify (OECD, 2021[45]). Regulations, guidance and frameworks, such as the OECD Principles on Artificial Intelligence, are increasingly put in place to guide the use and governance of AI systems in a safe, responsible and trustworthy manner (OECD, 2019[47]).

Box 3.3. Use of artificial intelligence-based models for credit scoring: the case of Viet Nam

Algorithmic credit scoring solutions powered by AI and using Machine Learning (ML) models use massive amounts of traditional and alternative data sources referred to as 'big data'. These include conventional credit information, social media data, digital footprints, payment behaviour and other transactional data accessible through Open Banking data sharing initiatives.

AI-based credit scoring is being used in many countries across Southeast Asia in consumer finance markets, and Viet Nam is one of the foremost AMS in which the usage of such models is spreading rapidly (Lainez and Gardner, 2023[48]). Consumer finance was virtually non-existent in Viet Nam ten years ago and has succeeded to grow considerably thanks to efforts made by local credit institutions to attract and service unbanked borrowers, inter alia through the use algorithmic credit scoring. Viet Nam has an official public credit registry the Credit Information Centre (CIC), gathering data from 30.8 million citizens, and a smaller private one, Viet Nam Credit Information Joint Stock Company (PCB) formed by 11 local banks in 2007.

FinTech companies, such as FE Credit, a consumer lender subsidiary of VPBank, are supplementing the official credit ratings with alternative scoring methods based on algorithmic models and big data. In 2018, it launched $NAP, an automated lending platform that aims at achieving a 'fast and easy credit' experience for its clients in Viet Nam (Lainez and Gardner, 2023[48]). Such industry activity has the potential to promote financial inclusion of underbanked parts of the population, however, emerging risks for consumers related to data privacy and to possible bias or discrimination may also need to be accounted for.

Financial institutions in ASEAN markets are leveraging AI to enhance their ability to proactively manage and mitigate risks for their customers, ultimately contributing to their financial well-being and indirectly promoting financial inclusion by sustaining their participation in the formal economy. For example, AI-driven models are being used in AML transaction monitoring, online sexual exploitation of children transactions[2] detection, mule account detection, phishing transaction detection and card fraud detection (Box 3.4). These tools can contribute to the strengthening of the capacity of financial institutions to comply with anti-money laundering (AML) and countering the financing of terrorism (CFT) rules, while increasing the confidence and trust that customers have in their participation in the formal financial system.

Box 3.4. Strengthening transaction safety through AI tools promotes consumer trust: the case of AI-assisted mule account detection

So-called money mules are actors who transfer or move illegally acquired money on behalf of someone else, usually recruited by criminals' help launder proceeds derived from online scams and frauds, or crimes like human trafficking and drug trafficking. Money mules add layers of distance between crime victims and criminals through the use of unrelated consumer accounts to move money at the direction of third persons involved in a criminal activity, which makes it harder for law enforcement to accurately trace money trails.

Financial institutions in the Southeast Asian region, such as UnionBank in the Philippines, perform mule account detection using AI tools. Such tools are designed to get ahead of fraudsters and detect them early on, so that appropriate actions can be taken when account owners have knowingly or unknowingly had their accounts used by criminals. The use of AI tools is a shift from the traditional reactive, reports-based approach with no automated process to detect mules, which was only effective once the customers reported a scam.

The ML-based detection is based on the patterns observed on (a) account opening data and (b) transaction behaviour data. The initial detection rate for UnionBank in the Philippines has been 42% of true money mules at a low rate of false positives and with 90% accuracy on non-mules prediction. This particular model is built and validated on real production data and real scenarios, and has to be continuously fine-tuned. In terms of efficiency, when comparing the traditional approach against the AI-based mule detection tool, money mule accounts are reported and endorsed for investigation for approximately a month after account opening, while the AI model has the capability to detect true money mules as early as four days after the account is opened.

Such models can support and enhance fraud prevention in an efficient way, while fostering customer engagement and promoting trust in formal financial services. The tools aim at protecting from fraud, accelerating investigation and providing an interface to view and analyse predicted mule activities, integrated into existing systems without disruption and through a transferable model and methodology which ensures reduced implementation time and effort.

Notes

[1] In addition to existing tools to promote fractional ownership in certain asset classes, such as real estate, for example, where REITs are a popular vehicle for retail participation.

[2] The model can monitor financial transactions to identify patterns and characteristics associated with child exploitation through payments to illegal websites then later can be flagged as suspicious transactions.

4 Policy considerations

The development of digital finance activity has followed a pattern of constant growth both globally and regionally in Asia. The COVID-19 pandemic has accelerated and intensified the digitalisation trend in financial markets with an increase in both offer and demand for digital financial solutions (OECD, 2021[27]) (OECD, 2022[49]). Digitally-enabled financial services and products, in the payments sector in particular, helped economies avoid a complete standstill during the COVID-19 pandemic, and they have the potential to support a digitally-enabled recovery.

Policymakers in the ASEAN region have embraced digital innovation as an important lever to accelerate economic development and to gain a competitive edge. At the same time, policy efforts are underway in ASEAN and globally to address challenges stemming from particularly challenging and risky areas of digital finance, such as crypto-assets and DeFi, and to mitigate ensuing risks to investors, consumers and the markets.

4.1. A rapidly evolving regulatory framework for DeFi and crypto-asset activity to mitigate risks and protect investors and markets

DeFi and crypto-asset activity can involve the non-compliant operation of certain crypto-asset market players, offering regulated financial activities and products, and/or the operation of other players outside the regulatory perimeter, depending on the jurisdiction (OECD, 2022[3]). This exposes markets and their participants to significant risks that are usually addressed by consumer and investor protection rules in traditional financial services. A possible proliferation in crypto-asset activity could have implications for macroeconomic (IMF, 2023[50]) and financial stability (FSB, 2022[51]), in addition to risks for market integrity, prudential risks and risks to financial consumer/investors derived from crypto-assets (OECD, 2022[4]; OECD, 2022[3]; OECD, 2022[2]). Policymakers in ASEAN, and across OECD economies, have been seeking to ensure that safeguards are put in place to protect investors, consumers and markets from risks related to this activity.

ASEAN regulators and supervisors have been mindful of the significant risks involved in DeFi and crypto-asset activity and a number of policy actions have been implemented, are ongoing, or are planned in the region (Sonksen, 2021[52]) (Table 4.1). Malaysia, Thailand and Singapore, for example, have undertaken additional efforts to communicate their approach to investors and digital assets service providers, for instance, through guidelines.

At the regional level, Japan has already introduced its framework for stablecoins and crypto-assets (FSA Japan, 2023[53]), and Korea is in the process of introducing a comprehensive policy framework for these markets (FSC, 2023[54]).[1] In Europe, regulation on Markets in Crypto-Assets (MiCA) came into force in June 2023 and will take effect in June 2024 (EU, 2023[55]). At the national level, some policymakers are considering complementary regulation and supervision of decentralised finance (e.g. (Banque de France ACPR, 2023[56])). At the global level, efforts are underway at the G20 level by the Financial Stability Board (FSB) to promote a comprehensive regulatory and supervisory framework for crypto-assets, including 'global stablecoin' arrangements, which are necessary to maintain macroeconomic and financial stability (FSB, 2022[57]; FSB, 2023[58]). IOSCO has also published Policy Recommendations for Crypto and Digital

Assets (CDA) Markets and DeFi Policy Recommendations aiming to address market integrity and investor protection concerns arising from these markets by supporting greater consistency of regulatory frameworks and oversight in member jurisdictions (IOSCO, 2023[59]).

Table 4.1. Existing regulation of crypto-assets in ASEAN

Country	Associated Authorities	Regulatory treatment of crypto-assets
Brunei Darussalam	The Brunei Monetary Authority (AMBD)	Legal for trading/holding, not usable as tender
Malaysia	Malaysian Securities Commission, the Central Bank of Malaysia	Legal as a security, with a ban on ICOs but allowance of Initial Exchange Offering (IEOs)
Singapore	The Monetary Authority of Singapore (MAS)	Legal, explicit clear-cut regulation of crypto-assets
Thailand	Bank of Thailand	Legal, but with restrictions on the banking sector from their use, the most well developed and clear-cut regulation of crypto-assets
Philippines	The Central Bank of Philippines	Legal
Cambodia	The National Bank of Cambodia, Cambodian Securities and Exchange Commission, the National Police	Ambiguous, but effectively legal with restrictions placed only on banks
Indonesia	Indonesian Central Bank, An agency within the Indonesian Ministry of Trade	Legal for trading/holding, not allowed for payments
Lao People's Democratic Republic	The Bank of Laos	Not illegal for individuals per se but prohibitions have been placed on financial institution
Myanmar	Central Bank of Myanmar (CBM)	Ambiguous for individuals, with explicit restrictions on financial institution
Viet Nam	The State Bank, Ministries of Finance and Public Security	Legal to hold/trade, but explicitly banned as a payment tool

Note: As of June 2023.
Source: Adapted from (Sonksen, 2021[52]).

The FSB framework calls for effective and proportionate regulation, supervision and oversight of crypto-asset activity and recommends that authorities require crypto-asset firms to have in place and disclose: governance frameworks; risk management framework; and reporting and disclosure frameworks (FSB, 2023[58]). Authorities should have the appropriate powers and tools, and adequate resources, to regulate, supervise, and oversee crypto-asset activities and markets, including those firms combining multiple functions and activities that may be conflicting.

Figure 4.1. FSB High-level Recommendations for the Regulation, Supervision and Oversight of Crypto-asset Activities and Markets and "Global Stablecoin" Arrangements

Source: FSB (2023[58]), FSB Global Regulatory Framework for Crypto-asset Activities, https://www.fsb.org/2023/07/fsb-global-regulatory-framework-for-crypto-asset-activities/

Institutional preparedness and co-ordination are two areas that may require particular attention by ASEAN policymakers for the implementation of the global policy frameworks for crypto-assets. In terms of preparedness, building institutional capacity for policymakers in AMS will be crucial for effective oversight of decentralised finance markets. In terms of co-ordination, ASEAN authorities will need to co-ordinate with each other at the domestic level to avoid fragmentation of oversight. AMS authorities will also need to co-ordinate at the international level both for information sharing and for supervision of crypto-asset and DeFi activity, which is inherently global by nature and is likely to require co-operation at the oversight level.

Co-ordination at the international level is one of the most critical areas going forward for decentralised finance markets. This is warranted given the speed at which these markets evolve and the rapid speed of development of new activities in these markets. International co-operation and co-ordination will protect against regulatory arbitrage and allow for consistency in regulatory and supervisory outcomes. Any lack of consistency in the application of the global frameworks and recommendations could result in a race to the bottom by regulators in countries with less strict frameworks, while opening the door for regulatory arbitrage by the industry. This will need to include both timely policy reaction in cross-border situations, as well as efficient information sharing between relevant authorities.

4.2. Policies to support a safe digital transformation and the development of FinTech that can contribute to financial inclusion

Although currently crypto-assets and DeFi are associated with significant risks for markets and their participants, appropriately regulated and supervised crypto-asset providers could in the future be beneficial contributors to the financial market ecosystem. Regulated and compliant stablecoins, for example, could provide an alternative for lower-cost international remittances, an important part of certain AMS financial systems (e.g. the Philippines). Traditional financial market participants may adopt decentralised finance technologies and practices (e.g. atomic settlement of securities or post-trade/clearing disintermediation) to capture potential efficiencies and productivity gains in financial market infrastructure. Robust comprehensive policy frameworks for these activities and markets are necessary to achieve such policy objectives, while they also provide the legal certainty necessary for the industry to reap the benefits of decentralised finance.

Over the past five years, ASEAN policymakers have indeed implemented a wave of reforms to address the digital transformation in financial markets. These reforms typically seek to simplify regulatory regimes to encourage new entrants – entrants that could reach new customers, offer new products, and provide cheaper and faster services – while simultaneously attempting to mitigate risks to the financial system. Since 2020, six AMS (Indonesia, Lao PDR, Malaysia the Philippines, Singapore, and Viet Nam) have introduced new or adjusted rules to govern e-money and e-payment service providers. Thailand has also established rules to govern e-payment service providers, with the introduction of its Payment Systems Act (PSA) in 2017. The use of e-wallets and QR codes for payments in ASEAN is also growing rapidly. Four AMS (Malaysia, the Philippines, Singapore, and Thailand) have recently established a licensing framework for digital banks and have begun pilots in this area. AMS and in particular Cambodia, Indonesia, Thailand, and Singapore are very active in experimentation and pilots of CBDCs.

Policymakers in ASEAN could also consider supporting the safe development of other FinTech applications that could be beneficial for the promotion of financial inclusion, fostering the safe and responsible digital transformation of their markets. This is particularly important when it comes to underserved MSMEs in the region, struggling to access finance. The promotion of the safe use of digital tools as enablers of MSMEs financing in a safe and compliant manner could assist in unlocking capital for productive uses. Such digital tools include *inter alia* the use of artificial intelligence-based models for credit scoring of thin file clients, such as MSMEs without tangible assets or prior credit history; the use of machine learning applications by development banks granting credit guaranteed loans for fraud detection in the application and screening process; or the deployment of DLT-based finance, such as tokenisation, for capital formation, fractionalisation and for the promotion of efficiencies in capital markets that can benefit all market participants.

Digital finance-related policy frameworks need to carefully balance risks and opportunities. The promotion of digital finance tools as enablers of SME financing needs to be done in a safe and compliant manner, addressing any emerging risks, with a view to allow for the benefits of digitalisation while safeguarding consumers and markets. Innovation facilitators and regulatory sandboxes or other types of participation in public-private co-operation for pilots and experimentation are possible ways for supervisors to stimulate innovation in finance in a controlled manner, while benefitting themselves from interaction with applications of novel mechanisms and technologies (OECD, 2023[60]).

Harmonisation of policy approaches to FinTech in the ASEAN region could be considered as a means to encourage cross-border activity and support innovation at the regional level. Particularly given the diverse level of institutional capacity in the region, more regional and international dialogue could help AMS tap into broader and deeper expertise and to develop policies and instruments that can best support domestic priorities. Where resources allow, AMS could consider establishing units that monitor innovations in financial markets in the relevant authorities.

Investment in skills, training and capacity building is a prerequisite for the successful implementation of any policy in digital finance, both for users (MSMEs in particular) and for policymakers. Users, such as MSMEs, may be willing but not capable to move towards digitalisation, including for their financing needs. Support for the promotion of digital financial literacy is increasingly important to equip users for their digitalisation journey in finance (OECD, 2018[61]).

When it comes to policymakers, resources need to be deployed to keep pace with advances in technology. The upskilling of policymakers is increasingly important given the increasing technical complexity of digital innovation. Enforcement authorities in particular will need to be technically capable of supervising such innovative forms of finance and empowered to intervene when required, but also to enjoy the benefits of digital innovation in RegTech/SupTech applications. Possible capacity constraints may undermine the policy effort and reduce the effectiveness of any global co-ordination not only in terms of addressing current risks (e.g. FSB recommendations in the case of crypto-assets) but also in terms of taking advantage of the benefits of digitalisation in finance.

Nevertheless, FinTech on its own is no panacea, particularly for financial inclusion objectives, and policymakers should also aim at the promotion of efforts in traditional finance. These include, inter alia, infrastructure development where necessary to reach remote areas, work on digital identification by the government for the simplification of KYC checks and onboarding by both traditional and innovative financial institutions, but also the strengthening of traditional credit bureaus to support creditworthiness assessments. FinTech and conventional financial services need to co-exist and interoperate in the wider financial market ecosystem, and the various policy initiatives need to be co-ordinated in that sense.

Note

[1] The Financial Services Commission announced that the Act on the Protection of Virtual Asset Users was passed at the National Assembly's plenary session on June 30. The Act focuses on enhancing the protection of virtual asset investors by introducing the following key points: (i) the definition of "Virtual Asset," (ii) the definition of "Virtual Asset Service Provider" ("VASP"), (iii) the obligations and prohibitions of VASPs to protect investors, and (iv) the Financial Services Commission's ("FSC") authority to supervise and inspect VASPs. (FSC, 2023[54])

Annex A. Aggregate net flows across geographies

Figure A A.1. Cumulative aggregate net flows across geographies from each year

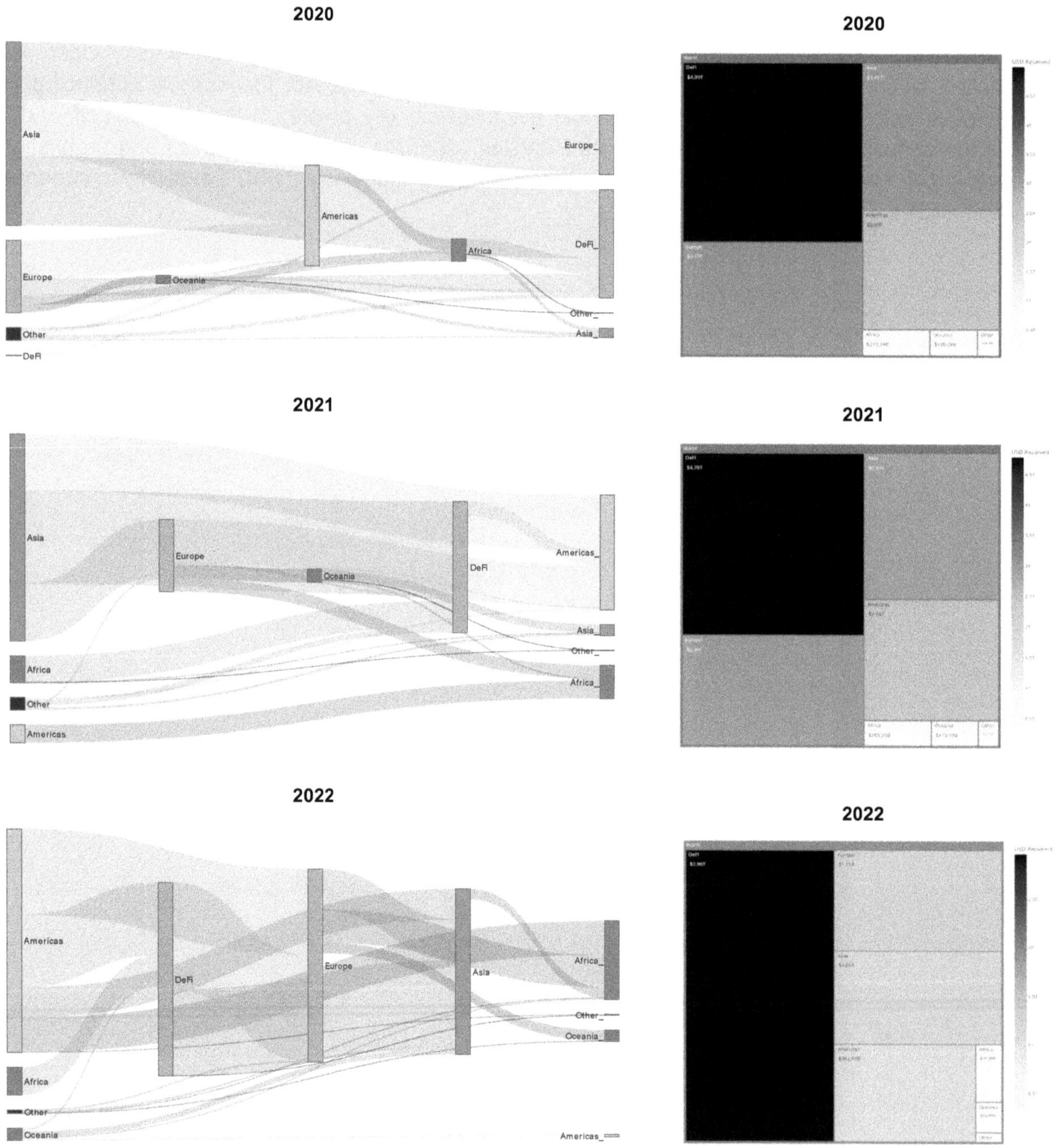

Annex B. Aggregate AMS Country data

Figure A B.1. Breakdown of crypto-asset activity by type of asset and Crypto-asset flows to Brunei Darussalam

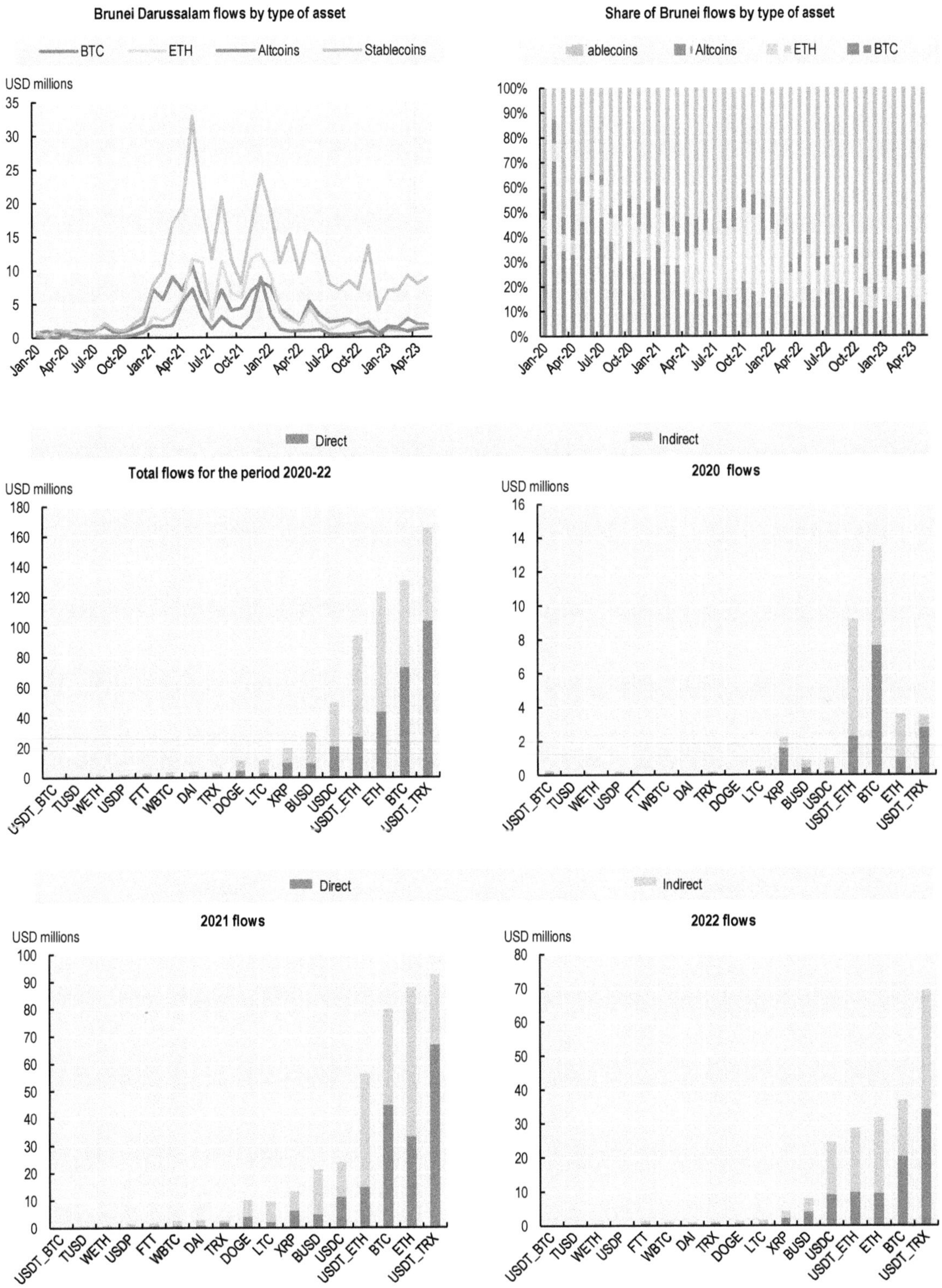

Source: Chainalysis and OECD staff Compilation.

Figure A B.2. Breakdown of crypto-asset activity by type of asset and Crypto-asset flows to Cambodia

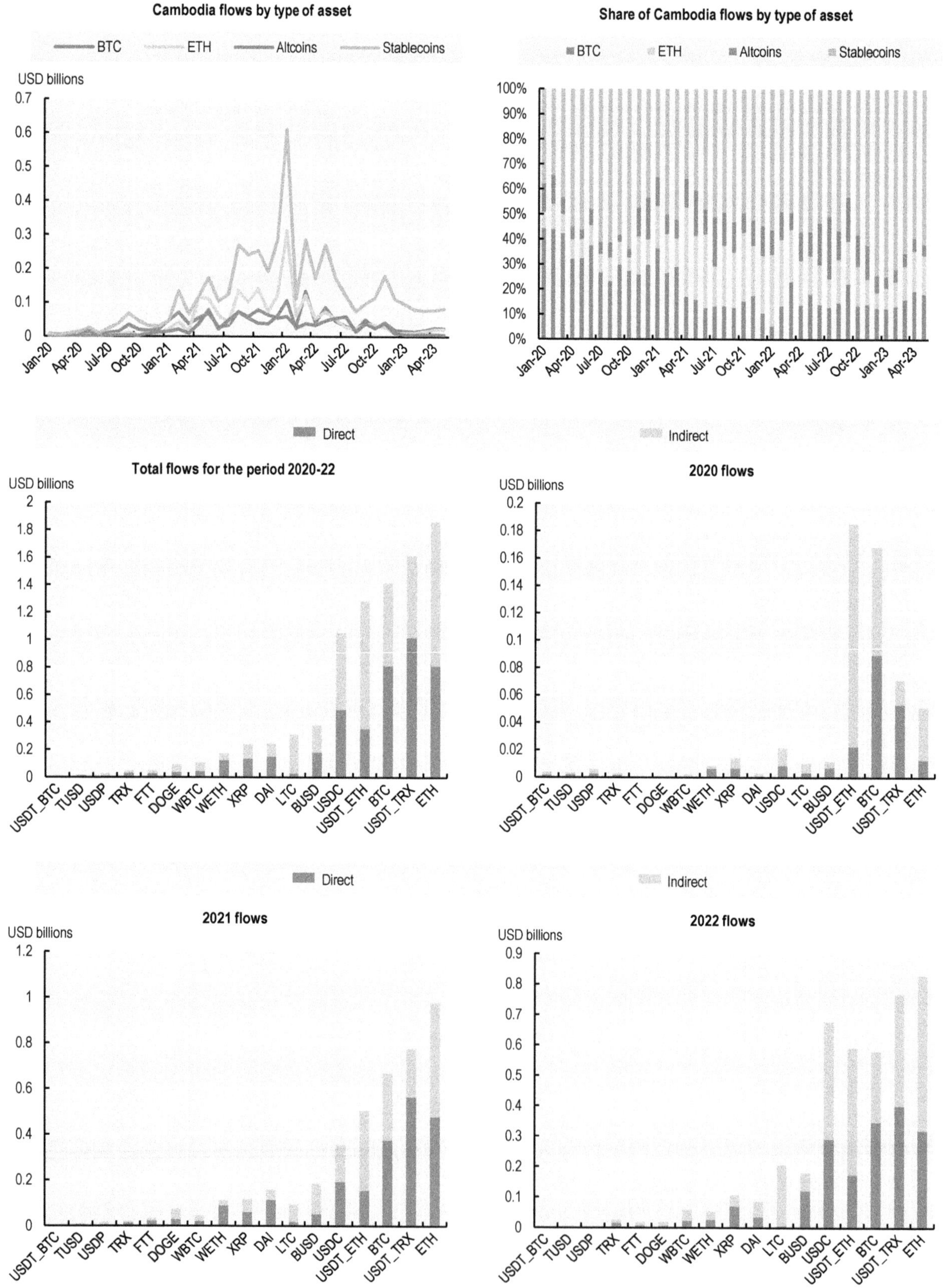

Source: Chainalysis and OECD staff Compilation.

Figure A B.3. Breakdown of crypto-asset activity by type of asset and Crypto-asset flows to Indonesia

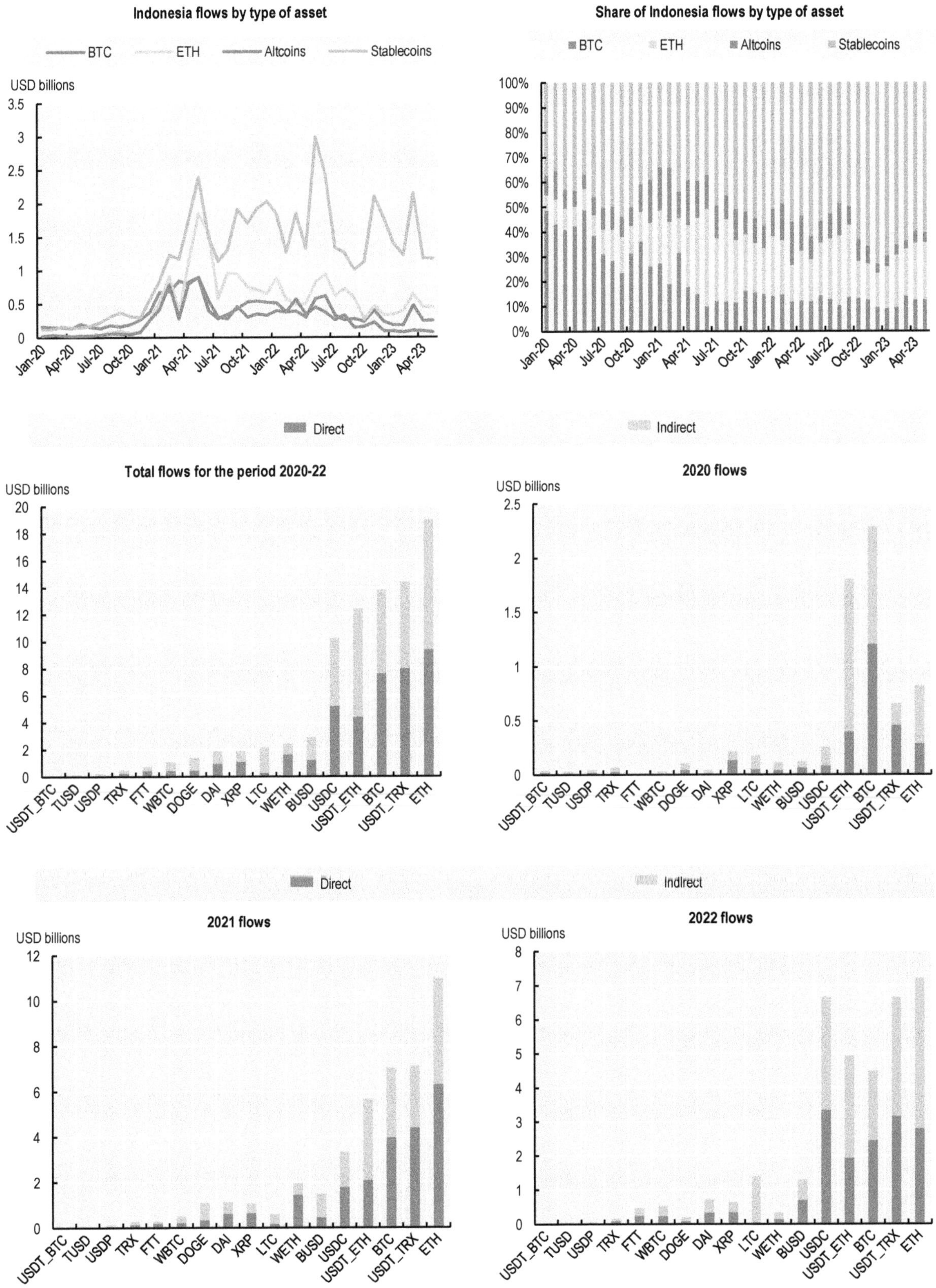

Source: Chainalysis and OECD staff Compilation.

Figure A B.4. Breakdown of crypto-asset activity by type of asset and Crypto-asset flows to Lao People's Democratic Republic

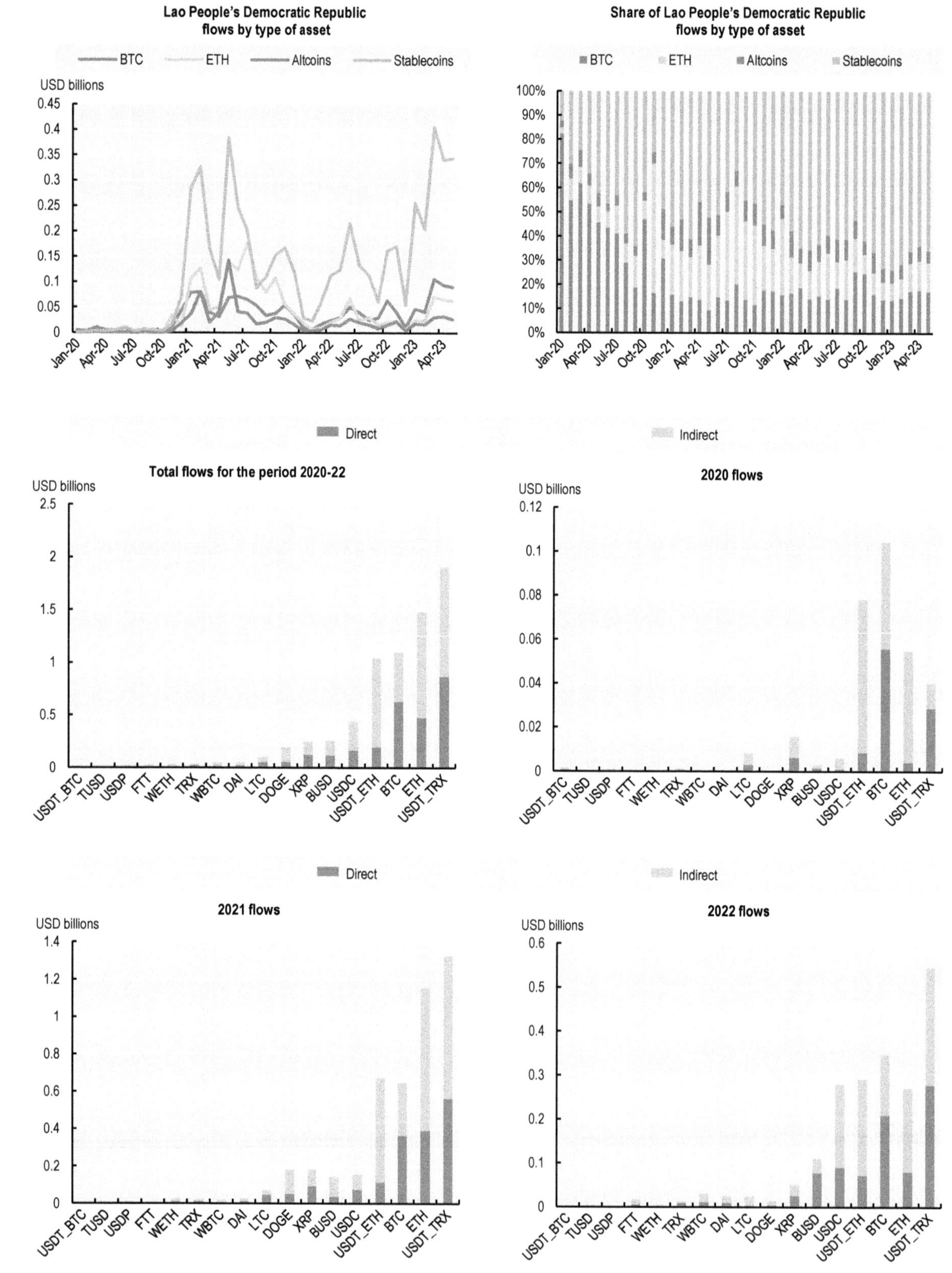

Source: Chainalysis and OECD staff Compilation.

Figure A B.5. Breakdown of crypto-asset activity by type of asset and Crypto-asset flows to Malaysia

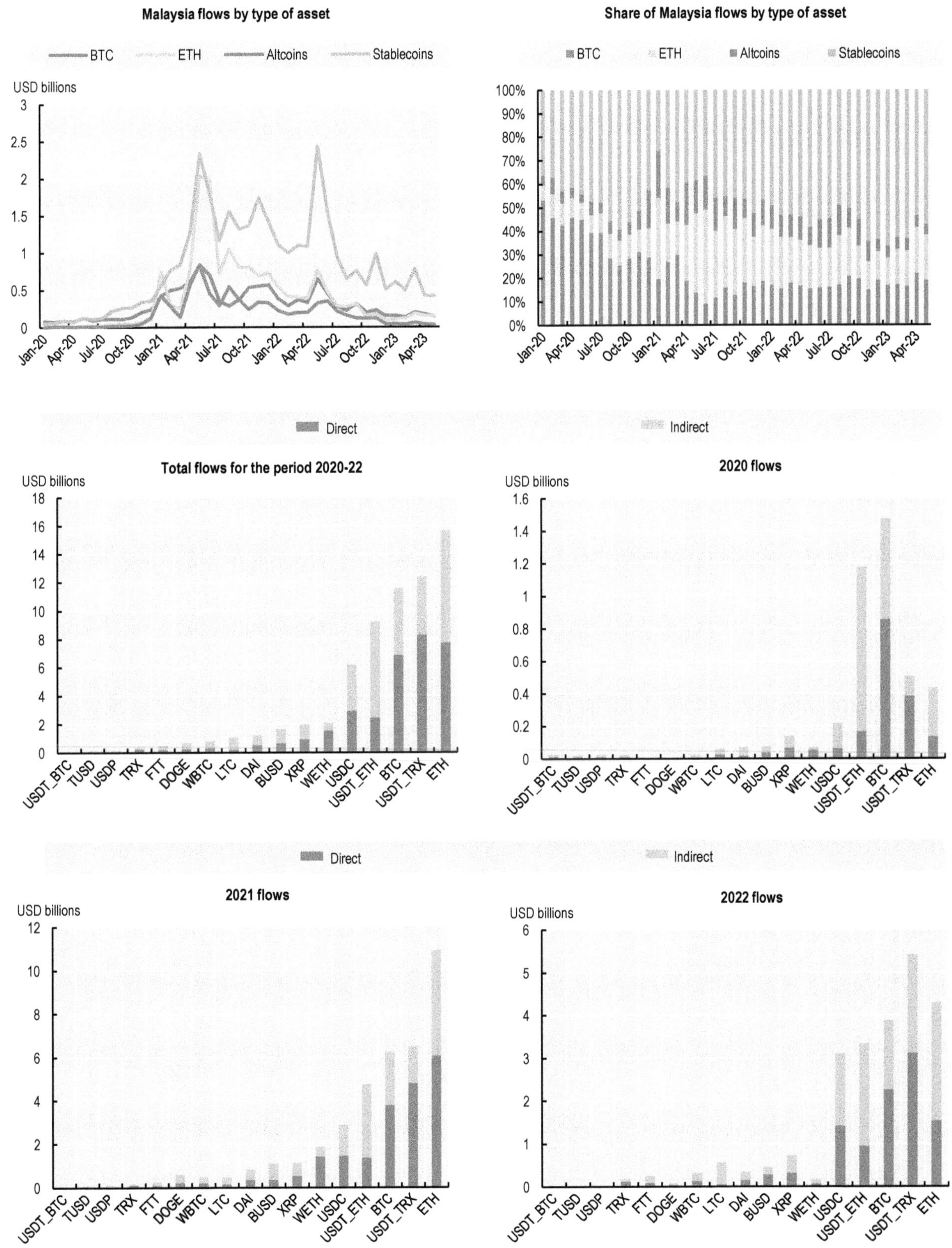

Source: Chainalysis and OECD staff Compilation.

Figure A B.6. Breakdown of crypto-asset activity by type of asset and Crypto-asset flows to Myanmar

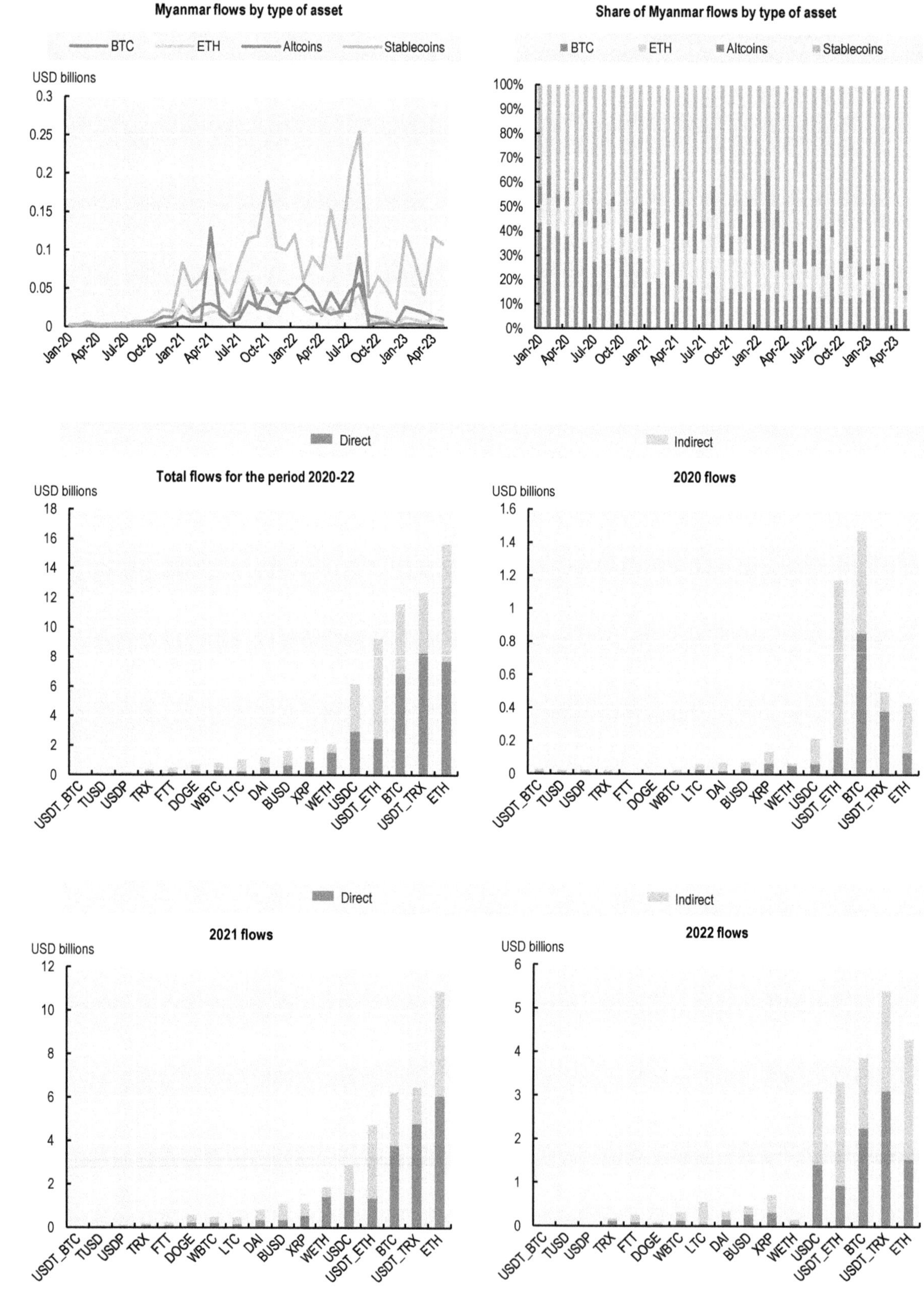

Source: Chainalysis and OECD staff Compilation.

Figure A B.7. Breakdown of crypto-asset activity by type of asset and Crypto-asset flows to Philippines

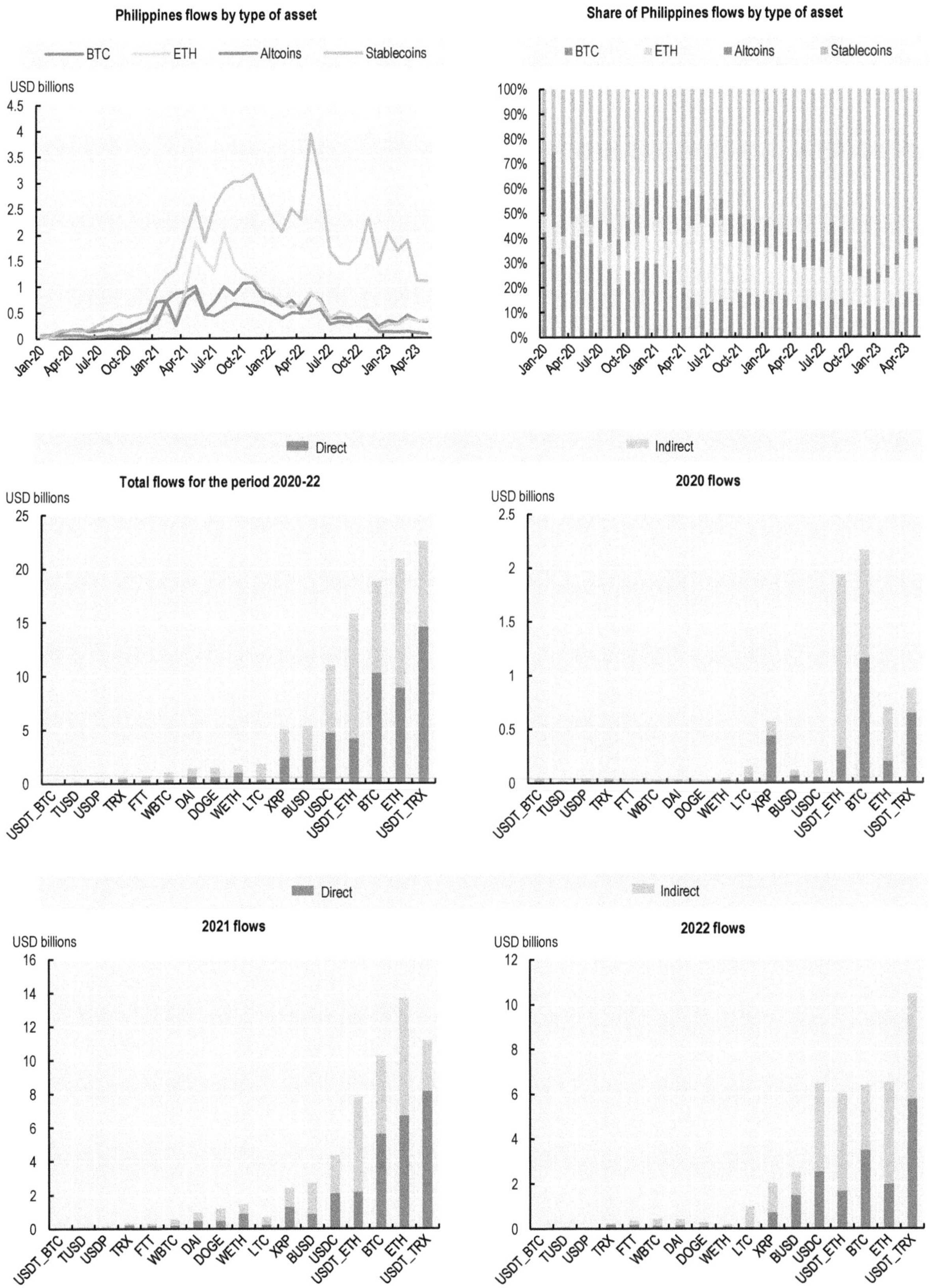

Source: Chainalysis and OECD staff Compilation.

Figure A B.8. Breakdown of crypto-asset activity by type of asset and Crypto-asset flows to Singapore

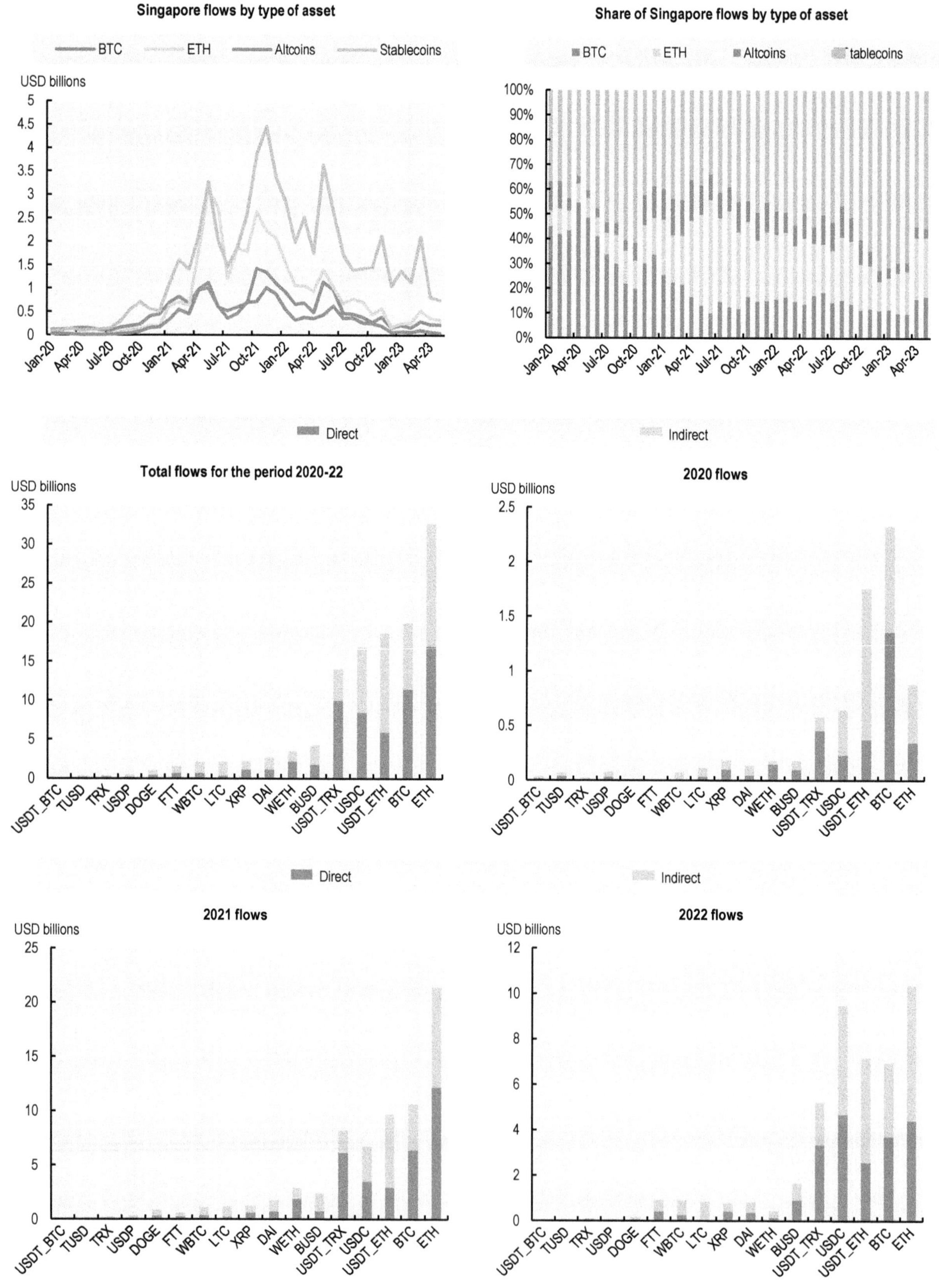

Source: Chainalysis and OECD staff Compilation.

Figure A B.9. Breakdown of crypto-asset activity by type of asset and Crypto-asset flows to Thailand

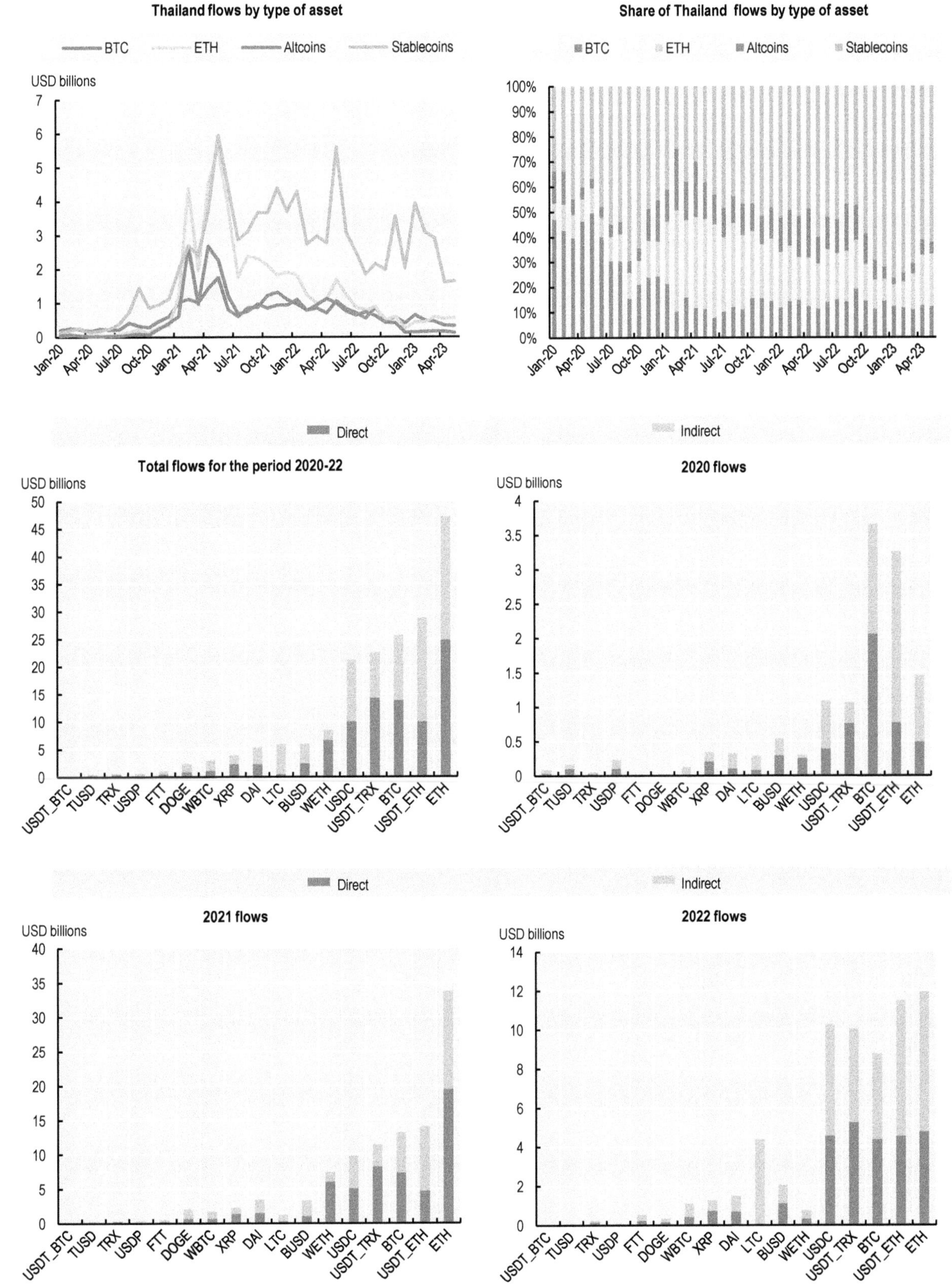

Source: Chainalysis and OECD staff Compilation.

Figure A B.10. Breakdown of crypto-asset activity by type of asset and Crypto-asset flows to Viet Nam

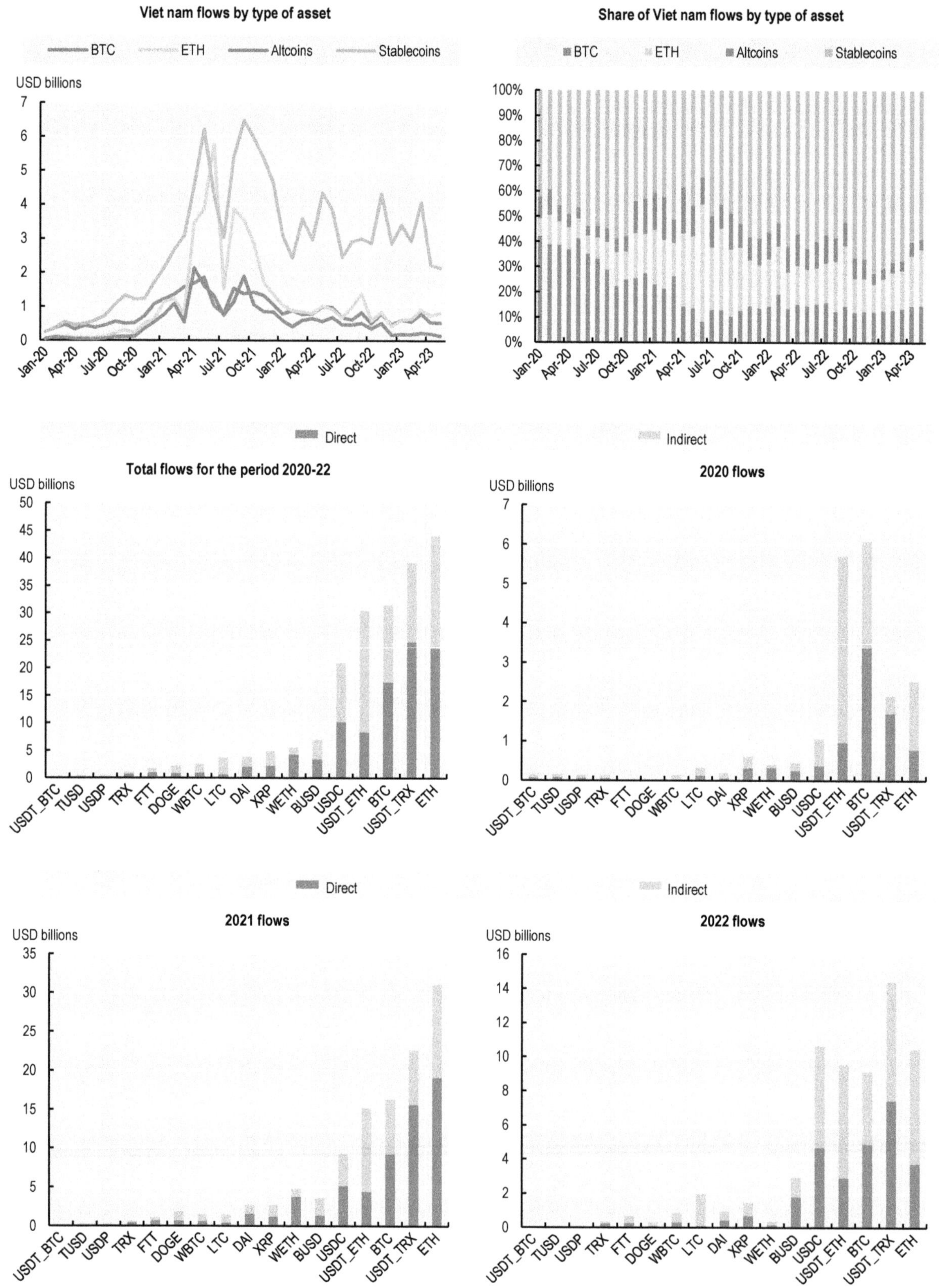

Source: Chainalysis and OECD staff Compilation.

References

Albanesi, S. and D. Vamossy (2019), "Predicting Consumer Default: A Deep Learning Approach", *SSRN Electronic Journal*, http://arxiv.org/abs/1908.11498 (accessed on 8 June 2021). [43]

Aramonte, S. et al. (2022), "BIS Bulletin No 57 DeFi lending: intermediation without information?", http://www.bis.org (accessed on 31 January 2024). [23]

ASEAN (2021), *ASEAN digital integration index*, https://asean.org/wp-content/uploads/2021/09/ADII-Report-2021.pdf (accessed on 15 June 2023). [1]

Auer, R., J. Frost and J. Vidal (2022), "BIS Bulletin No 58 Miners as intermediaries: extractable value and market manipulation in crypto and DeFi", http://www.bis.org (accessed on 31 January 2024). [16]

Bank of Italy (2019), *Corporate default forecasting with machine learning*. [42]

Banque de France ACPR (2023), *"Decentralised" or "disintermediated" finance: what regulatory response? | ACPR*, https://acpr.banque-france.fr/en/decentralised-or-disintermediated-finance-what-regulatory-response (accessed on 8 January 2024). [56]

BIS Innovation Hubs (2023), *Project Mariana: CBDCs in automated market-makers*, https://www.bis.org/about/bisih/topics/cbdc/mariana.htm (accessed on 6 July 2023). [30]

Bloomberg (2022), "Jump Report Shows Big Investors Exited Terra While Retail Bought - Bloomberg", https://www.bloomberg.com/news/articles/2022-06-03/jump-crypto-says-terra-was-a-losing-game-for-retail-investors (accessed on 26 October 2022). [21]

Carey, R. (2023), *Whales vs. Retail: Who's Using Curve? | by Riyad Carey | Kaiko*, https://blog.kaiko.com/whales-vs-retail-whos-using-curve-2ee09a998d94 (accessed on 25 July 2023). [19]

CCAF and ADBI (2019), "The ASEAN FinTEch Ecosystem Benchmarking Study", https://www.jbs.cam.ac.uk/wp-content/uploads/2020/08/2019-ccaf-asean-fintech-ecosystem-benchmarking-study.pdf (accessed on 13 February 2023). [41]

Chainalysis (2022), *2022 Geography of Cryptocurrency Report*, https://go.chainalysis.com/geography-of-crypto-2022-report.html?utm_campaign=Thread&utm_source=twitter&utm_medium=OrganicSocial (accessed on 18 June 2023). [8]

Chow, Y. and K. Tan (2022), "Is tokenization of real estate ready for lift off in APAC?", *Journal of Property Investment and Finance*, Vol. 40/3, pp. 284-290, https://doi.org/10.1108/JPIF-10-2021-0087/FULL/PDF. [33]

Cornelli, G. et al. (2023), "BIS Bulletin No 69 Crypto shocks and retail losses", http://www.bis.org/publ/work1049_data_xls.xlsx. (accessed on 31 January 2024). [22]

ECB (2022), "Study on the payment attitudes of consumers in the euro area (SPACE) – 2022", https://doi.org/10.2866/25551. [25]

Elliptic (2022), *Lazarus Group Identified as Behind $540m Ronin Bridge Heist*, https://www.elliptic.co/blog/540-million-stolen-from-the-ronin-defi-bridge (accessed on 18 June 2023). [12]

EU (2023), "Regulation of the European Parliament and of the Council on markets in crypto-assets". [55]

Finder (2022), *NFT gaming statistics - finder.com*, https://www.finder.com/nft-games-statistics (accessed on 18 June 2023). [13]

Forbes Advisor (2023), *What Is DeFi? Understanding Decentralized Finance – Forbes Advisor*, https://www.forbes.com/advisor/investing/cryptocurrency/defi-decentralized-finance/ (accessed on 3 July 2023). [18]

Fortune.my (2018), *All about Bitcoin Mining in Malaysia - Fortune.My*, https://www.fortune.my/ethereum-crypto-bitcoin-mining-malaysia.htm (accessed on 8 January 2024). [15]

FSA (2023), *FSA's Participation in MAS's "Project Guardian" initiative on Digital Assets*, https://www.fsa.go.jp/en/news/2023/20230626.html (accessed on 6 July 2023). [32]

FSA (2019), *Financial Instruments and Exchange Act : Financial Services Agency*, https://www.fsa.go.jp/en/policy/fiel/index.html (accessed on 6 July 2023). [38]

FSA Japan (2023), "Regulating the crypto assets landscape in Japan". [53]

FSB (2023), *FSB finalises global regulatory framework for crypto-asset activities - Financial Stability Board*, https://www.fsb.org/2023/07/fsb-finalises-global-regulatory-framework-for-crypto-asset-activities/ (accessed on 19 July 2023). [58]

FSB (2022), "Assessment of Risks to Financial Stability from Crypto-assets", http://www.fsb.org/emailalert (accessed on 18 February 2022). [51]

FSB (2022), *FSB proposes framework for the international regulation of crypto-asset activities - Financial Stability Board*, https://www.fsb.org/2022/10/fsb-proposes-framework-for-the-international-regulation-of-crypto-asset-activities/ (accessed on 12 July 2023). [57]

FSC (2023), *FSC Unveils Work Plan for 2023*, https://www.fsc.go.kr/eng/pr010101/79368?srchCtgry=&curPage=&srchKey=&srchText=&srchBeginDt=&srchEndDt= (accessed on 7 February 2023). [37]

FSC (2023), *Government to Ensure Virtual Asset User Protection, Transaction Transparency and Market Discipline*, https://www.fsc.go.kr/eng/pr010101/80317?srchCtgry=&curPage=&srchKey=&srchText=&srchBeginDt=&srchEndDt= (accessed on 17 July 2023). [54]

FT (2022), "Retail investors become vigilantes in hunt for crypto's most wanted man | Financial Times", https://www.ft.com/content/1a7d82ff-9986-4890-99e8-048940ce8553 (accessed on 26 October 2022). [6]

Fu, J. and M. Mishra (2020), "The Global Impact of COVID-19 on Fintech Adoption", *Swiss Finance Institute Research Paper Series*, https://ideas.repec.org/p/chf/rpseri/rp2038.html (accessed on 3 July 2023). [28]

Gambacorta, L. et al. (2019), *BIS Working Papers No 834 How do machine learning and non-traditional data affect credit scoring? New evidence from a Chinese fintech firm*, http://www.bis.org (accessed on 26 August 2020). [44]

IMF (2023), *Elements of Effective Policies for Crypto Assets*, https://www.imf.org/en/Publications/Policy-Papers/Issues/2023/02/23/Elements-of-Effective-Policies-for-Crypto-Assets-530092 (accessed on 12 July 2023). [50]

IOSCO (2023), "Policy Recommendations for Crypto and Digital Asset Markets Final Report", http://www.iosco.org (accessed on 8 January 2024). [59]

Knowledge Partners (2022), *Axie Infinity: How A Blockchain game is spreading Financial Inclusion*, https://ventureintelligence.blogspot.com/2022/02/axie-infinity-how-blockchain-game-is.html (accessed on 18 June 2023). [10]

Lahajnar, S. and A. Rožanec (2020), "The correlation strength of the most important cryptocurrencies in the bull and bear market", *Investment Management and Financial Innovations*, Vol. 17/3, pp. 67-81, https://doi.org/10.21511/IMFI.17(3).2020.06. [17]

Lainez, N. and J. Gardner (2023), "Algorithmic Credit Scoring in Vietnam: A Legal Proposal for Maximizing Benefits and Minimizing Risks", https://doi.org/10.1017/als.2023.6. [48]

MAS (2022), *Project Guardian*, https://www.mas.gov.sg/schemes-and-initiatives/project-guardian (accessed on 6 July 2023). [31]

Monetary Authority of Singapore (2020), "A Guide to Digital Token Offerings". [40]

Monetary Authority of Singapore (2017), *MAS clarifies regulatory position on the offer of digital tokens in Singapore*, https://www.mas.gov.sg/news/media-releases/2017/mas-clarifies-regulatory-position-on-the-offer-of-digital-tokens-in-singapore (accessed on 31 July 2019). [39]

Nassr, I. (2022), *Not-so-stable coins: A double-edged sword for decentralised finance and the key bridge linking DeFi to TradFi – On the level*, https://oecdonthelevel.com/2022/05/30/not-so-stable-coins-a-double-edged-sword-for-decentralised-finance-and-the-key-bridge-linking-defi-to-tradfi/ (accessed on 29 July 2022). [7]

news1.kr (2022), "Inspection and Investigation of State Administration 2022 (국감현장]정무위, 테라 국감 불출석한 증인에 "동행명령 검토")", https://www.news1.kr/articles/4842019 (accessed on 26 October 2022). [5]

OECD (2023), *Supporting FinTech Innovation in the Czech Republic: Regulatory Sandbox Design Considerations*, OECD Publishing, Paris, https://doi.org/10.1787/081a005c-en. [60]

OECD (2022), "Environmental impact of digital assets: Crypto-asset mining and distributed ledger technology consensus mechanisms", *OECD Business and Finance Policy Papers*, No. 16, OECD Publishing, Paris, https://doi.org/10.1787/8d834684-en. [14]

OECD (2022), "Institutionalisation of crypto-assets and DeFi–TradFi interconnectedness", *OECD Business and Finance Policy Papers*, No. 01, OECD Publishing, Paris, https://doi.org/10.1787/5d9dddbe-en. [4]

OECD (2022), "Lessons from the crypto winter: DeFi versus CeFi", *OECD Business and Finance Policy Papers*, No. 18, OECD Publishing, Paris, https://doi.org/10.1787/199edf4f-en. [3]

OECD (2022), *The FinTech Ecosystem in the Czech Republic*, OECD Publishing, Paris, https://doi.org/10.1787/068ba90e-en. [49]

OECD (2022), *Why Decentralised Finance (DeFi) Matters and the Policy Implications*, OECD, Paris, https://www.oecd.org/daf/fin/financial-markets/Why-Decentralised-Finance-DeFi-Matters-and-the-Policy-Implications.pdf (accessed on 18 February 2022). [2]

OECD (2021), *Artificial Intelligence, Machine Learning and Big Data in Finance: Opportunities, Challenges and Implications for Policy Makers*, OECD, Paris, https://www.oecd.org/finance/financial-markets/Artificial-intelligence-machine-learning-big-data-in-finance.pdf (accessed on 22 August 2022). [45]

OECD (2021), *Digitalisation and Finance in Asia - OECD*, https://www.oecd.org/finance/financial-markets/digitalisation-and-finance-in-asia.htm (accessed on 1 February 2023). [27]

OECD (2020), *Alternative financing instruments for ASEAN SMEs*, OECD, Paris, https://www.oecd.org/finance/alternative-financing-instruments-for-ASEAN-SMEs.htm (accessed on 6 July 2023). [36]

OECD (2020), "The Tokenisation of Assets and Potential Implications for Financial Markets", *OECD Blockchain Policy Series*, OECD, Paris. [24]

OECD (2019), *Artificial Intelligence in Society*, OECD Publishing, Paris, https://doi.org/10.1787/eedfee77-en. [47]

OECD (2018), "G20/OECD INFE Policy Guidance Digitalisation and Financial Literacy", OECD, Paris, http://www.oecd.org/going-digital (accessed on 19 December 2022). [61]

Okanurak, W. and S. Koohasaneh (2018), "Emergency decree on digital asset business B.E. 2561 (2018)", p. 8010, http://www.linklaters.com (accessed on 6 July 2023). [34]

Securities Exchange Commission (2020), *SEC revises rules for real estate-backed ICOs to enhance investor protection mechanism*, https://www.sec.or.th/EN/Pages/News_Detail.aspx?SECID=8288 (accessed on 23 March 2023). [35]

Shah, N. and M. Latif (2022), *The Depegging of UST*, https://jumpcrypto.com/the-depegging-of-ust/ (accessed on 26 October 2022). [20]

Sonksen, C. (2021), “Cryptocurrency Regulations in ASEAN, East Asia, & America: To Regulate or Not To Regulate.”, *Washington University Global Studies Law Review*, Vol. 20/1, pp. 171-200, https://go.gale.com/ps/i.do?p=AONE&sw=w&issn=15466981&v=2.1&it=r&id=GALE%7CA660000570&sid=googleScholar&linkaccess=fulltext (accessed on 15 March 2023). [52]

Statista (2023), *Crypto ownership by country 2019-2023 | Statista*, https://www.statista.com/statistics/1202468/global-cryptocurrency-ownership/ (accessed on 18 June 2023). [9]

Time (2022), “Axie Infinity Has Left Filipino Gamers Despondent + In Debt | TIME”, https://time.com/6199385/axie-infinity-crypto-game-philippines-debt/ (accessed on 18 June 2023). [11]

UOB, PWC and S. Association (2022), *FinTech in ASEAN 2022: Finance, reimagined*, https://www.uobgroup.com/web-resources/global/restricted/uobgroup/techecosystem/fintech-in-asean-2022.pdf (accessed on 13 February 2023). [29]

US Treasury (2016), *Opportunities and Challenges in Online Marketplace Lending M a y 1 0 , 2 0 1 6.* [46]

WEF (2023), *Digital ASEAN | World Economic Forum*, https://www.weforum.org/projects/digital-asean (accessed on 15 June 2023). [26]

www.ingramcontent.com/pod-product-compliance
Ingram Content Group UK Ltd.
Pitfield, Milton Keynes, MK11 3LW, UK
UKHW051507290926
15471UKWH00008B/1482

9 789264 526891